Don't Line Their Pockets with Gold

(Line Your Own!)

A Small How-To Book on Living Large
By Madelyn Rubin

Many Thanks to My Contributors

My Husband, Ned, for his constant support and for editing this book;
Bill Hatchett of *A-Coin and Stamp* of Jacksonville, FL
for allowing us to
use his coins and himself for the cover photo;
To Tim, Bill's brother, who gave his permission
to include him in this book;
and, of course, Billy, who has given the opportunity for us to take a
peek into his very private life, and who made this book possible.

Please Note: The names of certain individuals have been changed in order to protect their privacy.

Cover Photo: Madelyn Rubin

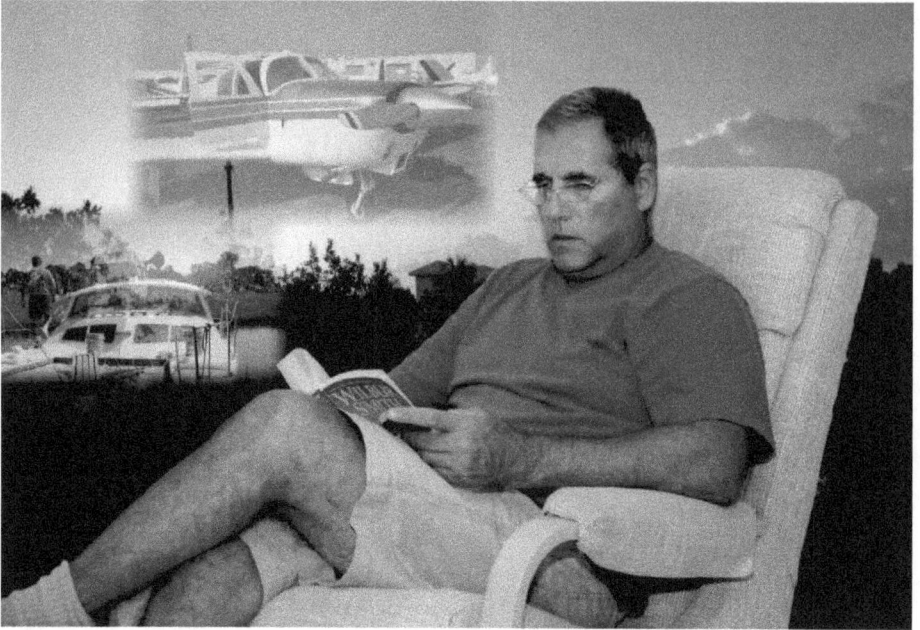

Billy in his Florida Keys Home

Madelyn Rubin

At this point in my life, I can finally look back and help others…help you….live a fuller life and retire with some gold in your own pocket rather than lining the pockets of others with gold. There are many ways to do this, a few how to books on the library and bookstore shelves, and even more on the web. There are many financial advisors too, but frankly, whenever someone has mentioned "financial advisor" to me in the past, I thought that I had to have a significant amount of finances to be advised about, before they would want to advise me. And I knew that I didn't fit in that category. So I decided to help you by telling you the story of my cousin, Billy. Why cousin, Billy? He asked the same thing. "I don't think anybody will be interested in my life, Mag (his nickname for me)," he said in his typical matter- of -fact manner.

I have admired Billy and his family for many years. Their closeness, support of each other, and, especially, Billy both enjoying life and having nice things, while rarely working a 9 to 5 job, has always intrigued me. What took me most by surprise was a situation that occurred about 12 years ago.

To give you a bit of background, Billy, born in 1953, has never been married and has never had children. About 12 years ago, his younger brother and informal business partner, Timmy, who was living in Atlanta, shared some horrible news with his family that his wife, Tamara, had just been diagnosed with an aggressive breast cancer. They had a darling two year old daughter and, of course, the entire family prayed and crossed their fingers while his wife received radiation and chemotherapy. Sadly, at the age of 34, his wife Tamara died, which left Timmy devastated. Eventually, he had gotten everything in order in Atlanta and returned to Jacksonville, Florida where the rest of his family was, and where he could get more family support. His mother, father, and sister lived together in Jacksonville and they invited Timmy and his two year old to come and live with them.

Billy, who lived a couple of miles away from the family home, could have chosen to provide only peripheral support, but he didn't. He jumped right in, like the rest of the family, and was there for Timmy and his little girl on a daily basis. He helped her get ready for pre-K every morning. He developed a special relationship with this little girl. She often responded to him like he was her mother, staying close and looking to Bill for approval. I know every other family member was very involved and helpful too, but Billy surprised me the most. While it seemed to me that he didn't want anyone depending on him, I was wrong. This family was practicing a lost art that many of our families practiced only a few generations ago: "Be as independent as you want, but if family needs you, come together and be there for them." Before I interviewed Billy for this book, I expected it must have been difficult for him to be like a second father or mother to his young niece. I was projecting my own issues. Never having had my own children, the responsibility for kids always scared me. I have fun around them, but never feel confident that I'm doing the right thing for them.

Anyway, after seeing Billy and his niece together and the independence that Billy and Timmy encouraged in their little girl, Jessie, it made me wonder what it would be like to be raised by two dads. How adventurous it would be to go out and try new things, without being held back by a worried, anxious mother (like my mother was, God rest her soul!)

Now back to our "How To" book. This is a book about how to look at, and interact with, the world, but in a very different way than is thrust upon us by the media, especially television and the Internet. This book presents a very different view and plan than the "how to" as dictated to us by Wall Street, Madison Avenue, and probably, our parents. It's about contentment, and how, even here in the United States, a person can still be without a 9 to 5 job, have no regular schedule, yet have everything she or he might desire. That's Billy. Billy, you see, owns houses (*really* owns them), owns a Mooney airplane, and owns a boat. He and his brother, Timmy, bought them in a way that anyone can learn. This book is about how Billy looks at life very differently than most of us. You probably wouldn't want to live exactly the way Billy does- I certainly don't. But, I have found dozens, yes dozens, of ideas while writing this book that I have adopted for myself and my family, while learning more about how Billy lives.

Billy is the most matter-of-fact person I know. Besides really owning homes, planes and boats, he eats out regularly, plus pays his taxes (begrudgingly.) Every time I talk to Billy, he has either just come back from a travel adventure or is buying a boat or is refurbishing an airplane or getting ready to go on another trip. You would think Billy is among the very wealthy, the way I have described him. In fact, it would have been easy to be as independent as Billy, on the farm, 100 years ago here in America. But Billy doesn't live on a farm. And it's the 21st Century. So how does he do it?

It isn't so easy to maintain a budget these days, not with advertising and mass media everywhere (Thank you Mr. /Ms. Banker, Madison Avenue, and Wall Street.) They dictate to us many of the items we "need," how we should live, and how we absolutely can't do without this or that special product or service. They have convinced most of us. We *deserve* that shiny *new* car, that *bigger, newer* house, *the latest* style of clothes, to feel good about ourselves in society. It's so exciting to share with all of our family, friends, and colleagues at work that new car we bought… at least for a few days, until the first payment is due. It's so exciting to buy that new home. And then, of course, we must change it to suit our tastes and buy new things to furnish or embellish it. It's *no problemo* if we don't have the money to pay for it now. Banks will happily loan us the money for those big items if we qualify (i.e. if we haven't screwed ourselves already by overextending our finances, which, of course, many of us have), and any store will happily accept our store credit cards----deferred payments and getting high interest rates mean big money for them.

That's the big "CC"-- Credit Cards. Before the recent Great Recession, cards were offered everywhere, from every bank or credit union, to anyone who could, or couldn't, afford them. And they're making a comeback (like the monster who wouldn't die) as the economy starts to improve. Banks and their investors make money on these "Loan Cards" in many ways: user charges to the merchant, cash flow and interest, ("the Float") to name a few. For example, a major bank sent me an offer for a credit card, every week, for five years! I called and emailed them many times, asking them to stop sending offers; told the rep that taking me off of their list would save them a bit of money and also save several trees. That was a joke--after I called them several times, I started getting *two* offers from them every week.

If you own a credit card, and your interest rate is 15% per annum on a card and your average balance is $4000 for example, the additional charge of interest to you for that year only is $600. $600!!! What else could you do with $600 other than lining the pockets of investors, banks, foreign entities and credit card companies with all of your money?

In her article *How Banks Make Money Off Of Credit Cards*, Gabriella Morrongiello notes: "These companies will squeeze in revenue by charging fees, soliciting warranties and advocating additional identity theft protection packages. According to CreditCards.com, the nine largest credit card issuers earned a combined profit of about $3.85 billion in 2010 from a total of more than 1 billion issued cards. Evidently, the credit card industry is doing a fine job at making money, even through their most responsible customers." (*The Daily Barometer*. Thursday, May 17, 2012.)

Back to Billy:

You might think that Billy robs banks, but he doesn't. Also, he doesn't steal from the rich or poor and he hasn't won the lottery. In our family, Billy and his brother Timmy seem to be the only ones that have managed to live the life they want instead of falling into a happenstance existence that just unfolded along the way. Even when Wrenches get tossed into his smoothly running life, as Wrenches are wont to do, he takes the wrench and uses it as a tool to better himself. Now, I hate a Wrench in the Works, and any surprise that changes my life in bad ways. I take the wrench personally. I bargain with it, try to throw it back, and claim that it's not *my* wrench- perhaps it was delivered to the wrong address. On the other hand, I believe that we're on this earth to learn how to handle Wrenches -- those inevitable surprises and unexpected changes that occur in our lives. Nietzsche's saying "That which does not kill us, makes us stronger" comes to mind, but it *feels* like it's going to kill me every time. Yet it turns out that he was right, most of the time....

Back to Billy and the wrench. I have the definite feeling that Billy does not see most changes in his life as "Wrenches" (except new government taxes and rules, but we all have an Achilles' heel.) That's one of the many things that I have learned from him—to see the wrench in your life as a tool and leverage to success, not as an obstacle.

I want to continue with a bit more of Billy's background. Billy's parents, Aunt Gemmel and Uncle George, have similar characteristics to my own family of origin. That's because Billy and his siblings are related to me from my mother's and father's side--my mother introduced her nephew, Uncle George, to her sister-in-law, Aunt Gemmel.

You couldn't find a more dissimilar background for a married couple (except, perhaps, for my mom and dad.) Aunt Gemmel and my dad, Louie Senior, were sister and brother, raised in a Lebanese, Catholic family. Their dad, Joe Keryakos, was a fun-loving, hardworking guy who owned a grocery store here in Jacksonville. His wife, Mary, our grandmother, was disowned by her father for marrying Joe, who was an employee of Mary's parents in Lebanon. These are the sorts of things that happened in Lebanon in the early 1900's. Mary chose Joe for love rather than marry a man 20 years older, that had been arranged for her. Billy's mother followed her heart in a similar way as her mother, Mary. While the family traditions here in America were steeped in the old ways of Lebanon, such as specific rules and roles for sons and daughters, Aunt Gemmel, the youngest of eight, broke out of that mold. She chose to do what her own mother did, rather than what her own mother said to do. Instead of being a housewife or working in the grocery store, she decided to go to nursing school at Saint Vincent's Hospital here in Jacksonville and become a

Registered Nurse. So, Billy's mother, Gemmel, chose her own path in life and was a model of independence for Billy.

Uncle George, whose ancestors were American pioneers and part of the vast Andrews family, came from a long line of Southerners. They were hard-working country folks with the values that came along with being in the South in the early 1900's, in a small town in North Florida, but with a significant difference. While many white folks in the area maintained a strong segregationist attitude, my grandfather - Billy's great, great grandfather (William [Bill] Andrews)-was different. By all accounts, he was genuinely kind to people of all races and persuasions, strangers and passersby, whom his neighbors would never consider helping. This is the way Billy is and so he inherited not only independence, but a social consciousness well ahead of its time. While many of the characteristics of these families are very different-- the Andrews family and the Lebanese Keryakos family-- they both have two very strong threads: independent thinking and an entrepreneurial spirit. Billy received both of these traits and has used them to the utmost in his life.

What I did to find out more about Billy was to interview him several times. He's quite a private person, so I had to do some Old World-style bargaining with him to get him to talk with me. For our first two interviews I drove to Billy's home in Jacksonville, Florida. He built this home from the ground up. It is close to the center of the city, yet nestled in the woods at the end of a short, suburban-like street. He left the woods thick and natural but open enough so that you can see the ravine from the giant windowed wall on the second story of his home. This is an older neighborhood, so there is no Homeowner's Association, with rules and regulations (Billy's Achilles' heel) and no quarterly or yearly fees. So, Billy has more *freedom* (a key word in his life) to do what he wants with his home and his land.

As you drive up to the fenced and gated land, all you see is an old car and a beat-up boat nestled in the North Florida vines and forest.

Vines and Forest of North Florida
Madelyn Rubin

Once you get through the gated driveway, and the thick woods, you see his two-story home. The style is a combination of rustic and contemporary. A good-sized screened porch stares out at you, like a lookout post, guarding the house and the property, as if protecting its inhabitants. When you walk up to the home, you first see what looks like a giant "under the house" garage. When you approach a bit closer, you see an array of tools and planks of wood, here and there, until you realize that it is actually a gigantic "under the house" workshop, fully equipped, with every shop tool imaginable. As you go into the door of the home and walk up the narrow, dark, quaint staircase, you get a feel for one of Billy's central philosophies right away: "Build it to last, not to win a *House Beautiful* contest." Yet, as a Certified Home Stager and Redesigner, I have thought many times that I could take this house and make it ready for *Southern Living, House Beautiful* or *The Energy Efficient Home* in a week… and for a few thousand bucks.

Billy's Self-built Home in the City
Madelyn Rubin

The second floor of Billy's home is the main floor, and has an open kitchen. The kitchen is fully equipped, but Billy only installed doors on most, but not all, of his kitchen cabinets. It might be because he didn't feel he needed them, or perhaps that they just took extra time to open, when you want to get something out of them real fast. I asked him several times why he didn't have doors on his kitchen cabinets. The response was something that was classic Billy: "Why, Mag (Billy's nickname for me) I can see whether I have an item way before I get to the cabinet. I can just be sitting in my family room and look. It saves me a lot of time searching for something."

This is a good time to address why Billy has no wife. It's a fair question. I know I wouldn't want to live without kitchen cabinet doors. I know many women who wouldn't want to live without kitchen cabinet doors. But Billy doesn't have to worry about anyone else's opinion of his house, because he is single. That doesn't mean that people haven't lived with him off and on. A few women have. It just means that only he owns the home, likes it that way, and can live and keep the place the way he wants.

Bill's Handmade Kitchen with Most of the Cabinet Doors
Madelyn Rubin

Does this mean you can't learn anything from his lifestyle if you have a spouse or partner? Absolutely not! I certainly wouldn't have spent all of this time writing this book if I hadn't learned so many valuable life skills and acquired so many tools from Billy, and I have been married to the same person for 21 years. It takes some serious, extra effort to explain the value of making changes to your spouse or partner, but the values have been worthwhile, TENFOLD, in my life, both as an individual and in marriage. Billy has chosen to forego the explanations to others and for him, it works.

If and when you make some of these changes, the Wall Street folks, like the banks, credit card companies, and the media, probably won't notice, unless a lot of us make a bunch of changes. But you'll notice and your family will notice. You'll have the chance to spend more time on other very important aspects of your life, like relationships, and time with friends and family, and hobbies, and volunteer work. In fact, you will find that you are enjoying life more and more. And you'll be one less person who is lining the pockets of Wall Street with your gold.

The First Interview with Billy – December, 2009

When I first interviewed Billy for this book, I talked with him for 20 minutes about how he can live so well, with so many of life's luxuries, without much money. While I was talking, I realized that he was working on something quite intently.

What are you stirring in that large pot, Billy? I asked.

"Making laundry detergent" *Billy replied, in his matter-of-fact way. Short and to the point. Avoid Needless Words. You get your answer and if you want more, you have to ask. Luckily, with Billy, I have learned to always ask for more information –which, I have noticed, sometimes encourages positive relationships with other, and sometimes results in negative ones. (A bit like a Mack truck myself, I usually don't find out about the negative stuff until my fellow brutally honest brother tells me months later that I have offended yet another person.)*

Oh, laundry detergent, I said, laughing. I had caught myself once again, asking questions about how he lives so well, so frugally, and yet there it was in front of me. I had merely to open my eyes and observe. So tell me how you're making it?

"I got the recipe from an engineer buddy of mine. It's pretty simple and dirt cheap. Have you ever heard of Napfa® Soap for taking out stains? Use a bar of that. Dissolve it in 5-6 cups of water."

How do you dissolve it? "

Warm up the water, take the bar of soap, then either grate it, or make it finer, so it dissolves in the water. Bring it to a boil, take it off the heat and make sure it is dissolved in the water. Add ½ cup of Borax® (which is $1.95) and a cup of Baking Soda, two dollars. Mix them all together with five gallons of water."

What are you mixing it in?

"A drywall bucket."

So that makes five gallons of liquid detergent! I replied, proud of my higher mathematics. Though it seems like a simple assumption, having been a REALTOR® for many years, I'm accustomed to mental math. But 5 gallons! What a huge amount for so little money!

"Um-hmm" Billy said.

Which lasts you for……..?

"It lasts me forever."

Six months? A year?

"Yep, it depends on how many dirty clothes I have."

Do you put a top on that container?

"Yeah."

So, Billy, you're OK with me doing this, right? It's okay if I ask you hundreds of questions about how you live, and so on?

"I don't mind you doing it, but I think you're kinda spinning your wheels. I don't think what I do is all that revolutionary."

Well, of course, you don't. That's because you do it all of the time. I'll take my chances, I said to Billy. *And then if we both get paid in the end...*

"I'll say. That's a smart girl! That girl is so smart; those people better buy another book!"

We both laughed.

(With formal training in psychology and clinical social work, I knew that Billy's childhood and upbringing influenced him strongly, and I wanted to find out more about this.)

(Note to the Reader: If you get lost regarding who is saying what, my comments, questions, and replies are in italics. Billy's answers and comments are in regular type).

Billy, I want to know about how you grew up. You were born in 1953. I know you lived in Jacksonville, Florida some, and in Miami and I know that Uncle George (Billy's father and my mother's nephew) was a woodshop teacher..."

"Dad taught Industrial Arts ...mainly drafting and stuff like that, at Fletcher High School in Jacksonville Beach, Florida. For extra income in the summers, I guess he would teach Woodshop, too. He might have done it all year. But his degree was mainly in drafting.

What is Industrial Arts?

"Well, he taught architectural drawing, engineering drawing, and stuff like that."

So you really followed in his footsteps in becoming an engineer.

"Engineering is totally different, but they use the same tools such as drawing."

You are a civil engineer?

Actually, a Mechanical Engineer.

So what's the difference?

"The basic difference is that Mechanical Engineers deal with stuff that is moving."(*Like airplanes and boats, of which Billy and his brother, Timmy, have much experience.*) "Civil Engineers design static things, like roads and buildings. Outside of that, we use pretty similar equations."

You told me one time that your Dad instilled more of a work ethic in y'all than you really would have liked.

13

"Oh, yeah," Billy said with his voice rising a pitch. "That's pretty true. I guess that's real true. There was always something at my childhood home that had to be done. Our extracurricular activities consisted of hoeing-out flower beds, stuff like that. We put a flower garden in, around the house, and by the time we got that done, the garden had to go all the way around the house again, then it had to get bigger and bigger. Never ending obstacles of life."

Is he the one that taught y'all how to build? I inquired. For as long as I can remember, since they have both been adults, Billy and Timmy have built various homes and sold them.

"I can't say nope entirely. Mainly books," Billy said.

When? After your engineering degree or before?

"After. I graduated from college in 1977 from the University of Florida."

Did your brother, Timmy, graduate from college?

"Nope."

Did you both work together to learn how to build homes? Or, did you, Billy, first read books, learned how to build, then taught Timmy and John?

We all pretty much read books and we then learned together." (John, by the way, is Billy and Timmy's eldest brother.)

Billy proceeded to tell me how his early career began and how he got into building homes.

"I went up to Detroit in 1978, and bought my first house. I worked for Ford Motor Company as a Mechanical Engineer and saved about $6 grand. I was in a 4 year program. They train you in different parts of the company because they want you to be well rounded and they want you to, eventually, go into management. One time I worked in Arizona on their proving grounds and cars, another time in Detroit, another time in their experimental garage. You get like 5 different assignments."

You got to actually do experiments?

"Yep. Working in specific areas of the company."

Hard Working, Ass Kicking, Uncle George (In his Less Ass-kicking Years)
Madelyn Rubin

How long did you work for them?

"I worked for 2 years and 9 months."

So you were able to save $6,000 during that time in the late 1970's.

"I bought a house in Detroit, paid $21,000 for it. It was a 1 bedroom, 1 bath. I bought the house after the first year and a half I was there. I paid it off before I left Detroit. Ford was having a tough time, like they had a few years ago during the Recession. They had to lay off a bunch of people. There were guys all around me losing their jobs. And I didn't really care if I had a job or not."

Did you have more money saved by then?

"It never takes me much money to live."

So you saved $6000 that first year?

"Year and a half" said Billy. "My income was $17,000/year."

So, you sold the house in Detroit?

"I kept the house and rented it out."

How much did you have saved by then? I'm trying to get an idea, because that's what your life's foundation was based on, right?

"I don't remember how much I saved. I've never saved less than 50% of my pay check."

So the first job Billy ever had, he made $17,000 gross a year and saved at least $7000 net. In a year and a half, he put $6,000 down on his first home. He would have had $10,500 total saved (1.5 years) minus $6,000 equaling $4500 still saved. He lived on about $7000 a year in 1978. In two years, that left him at least $8,000 saved even after he bought his first home.

Where did you put that 50%?

"In the bank, till I found a better investment."

In a Money Market account?

"No, I was too stupid at the time; just a savings account at the Credit Union."

When did you do a better investment? Did you find another house?

"Yep. I came back to Jacksonville and my parents bought that farmhouse in Northside, and it was a wreck. My brothers John and Timmy and I spent about a year and a half rebuilding it."

In the early '80s?

"Yep."

I remember this house well. While I hadn't spent much time with Billy's family in the past, there was always something about them that made me want to get to know them better. Maybe it was because I was related to them on both sides of my family. I figured we had a lot in common. Billy's family had lived in Miami for years and I was very excited to have them back in Jacksonville. "Maybe now I can get to know them better," I thought.

The home Uncle George and Aunt Gemmel bought was a giant 19th century farmhouse in the countryside of North Jacksonville. You had to go down a dirt road, take a fork in the road and, if you were lucky, you would find it. It welcomed you with its big, stately two story presence. We always went in through the backdoor, which lead to a porch. We had Keryakos family gatherings there because it was the only home that would hold all of us. The screened porch lead to the kitchen, which was always inhabited by the women of the Keryakos family, cooking or cutting up food or just sitting at the table, catching up on family news.

One of my professions for many years was as a REALTOR® and I have always loved to look at homes, especially historic homes, and it was continually exciting to go out to this home. As Billy said, it took him and his two brothers a year and a half to renovate it. Thus, every time I went to visit within that year and a half, there would be a surprise awaiting in one of the rooms: new gleaming wood floors, sparkling cobalt blue tiles in the bathroom, a unique wood nook in the kitchen. The home had a small family room and a large living room/dining room. I don't remember any of us spending much time in the living/dining room, though. We spent a lot more time in the small family room and even more time in the kitchen. Being a member of a Lebanese Catholic family, you don't get too far from the food and the food is usually in the kitchen.

So Billy, how did you live when you were remodeling your parents' historic home? You had your savings?

It didn't take anything to live then because I was rebuilding that house for my parents and I could live there. Matter of fact, they even paid for all the food.

That was the trade.

Yep.

By then, had you invested your savings somewhere else?

No, kept it in a savings account. I had about $10,000 at that time. By that time, I believe I'd paid off my house in Detroit. I put every bit of money I had to pay off that house. That was the last mortgage I had. I hated having a mortgage.

You hated having a mortgage because...?

There was no reason for it 'cause you're paying somebody else extra money. Not only that, when you have a mortgage, you have to have insurance.

I gasped intensely, *"You don't have insurance on this house!?!"* Then starting to think like Billy, *"If it burned down, you could just build it again."*

That's right. This house cost me $12,000. I built it in a year. No matter what I do it always takes me a year.

That's not so bad. Did Timmy help you build this house?

No. I built this one by myself. It cost me $12 or $13,000, not including the property.

Now, let's go back so that I can understand how you got that money. You had $10,000 and you were helping your parents build their home. It was a tradeoff with them for a year in a half. This was in 1982 thru 1984.

Timmy, my brother, was working at Century 21 Apartments at the time. He worked in the health club and I'd go in there on occasion. Actually, we had an apartment over there after we got finished with my parents' home. We met this guy named Joe Warner who worked at the Jax Electric Authority. He said they were looking for a Mechanical Engineer at JEA. I thought I would talk to them.

So you were just living on your savings at that time? $10,000.

Yep. Since Timmy worked at the club, he got an apartment for like ½ price. So it didn't really cost that much. We didn't have any furniture to speak of. As a matter of fact, our "IDA" stood for Interior Decorated Apartment. Friends called it "ITA" (long I), the interior apartment. They were being sarcastic.

How much was your rent? $200/month?

Billy nodded. "So I worked at the JEA for two years and tested their power plants."

"And never saved less than half of your paycheck" I replied, dazed and amazed that any human being living in the United States could do something so financially avant garde.

Billy added, "Oh yes, by then, I was making more money. I was making about $27,000."

By then it was adding up some. Because you could live on your living expenses of 50%, so the other 50% was adding up. And you were still keeping it in a savings account?

Yeah. And my expenditures were always the same, I never lived different. So when you have a bigger salary, it's climbing exponentially.

So how much of your salary did you save of that? 75% or 60%?

"It could be," Billy said in his matter of fact way. And Timmy decided he wanted to build a house and he wanted me to help him.

"The one in Jacksonville in Arlington?" I said, feeling a pinge of guilt that as a real estate agent I had tried to sell that house and couldn't sell it for the money we had initially, asked.

Yeah, the one off of Hidden Hills. Timmy and I talked about it for a while and after I worked at JEA for two years, then I went out on my own. You know, it seems that all of my jobs have been great jobs, and it isn't anything bad about the job, it's just me.

"Well, perhaps it's just not being independent," I chimed in. Being independent and doing what we want, when we want to, and the way we want to, is a family tradition on both sides of our families.

"Well you always have to work at a specific time, 8-5 or whatever, and I don't do that" Billy declared. After lunch, I get sleepy, and I don't want to make myself not take a nap if I want one, so I decided for my 30th birthday, I'd never work for anybody again. So, that was a birthday present. March 8, 1983, was my last day at JEA.

That's when you said "I'll never work for somebody else again."

"Actually, I didn't say that. I just felt like I never would again. I still have no qualms about working for somebody, just that I don't want to."

Did Timmy save the same way that you have? 50% or more of his salary?

Yep. I'd say he lives a real similar style.

So when y'all bought the land for that house, y'all shared equally?

Actually, my parents owned that piece of property in Arlington. He bought it from them, built it and we shared the profits with our parents. I think we held the mortgage on it and that's the way it sold. It worked out good.

What kind of profits did you make on it?

We sold it for about $100 grand. We bought the property for $15 grand cash. Materials were about $35,000 plus closing costs. Made about $45,000 and split it. So we had about $23,000 each. So then I had enough money then to build this house. Bought the land for $8,000, half an acre.

"Nobody would want this land the way it slopes," I said, having tried to sell sloping land in Florida when it had very little flat land attached to build on. The Army Corps of Engineers declares much land that is anywhere near water or swamp as environmentally protected, so it's quite difficult to get necessary permits.

"Matter of fact," Billy stated, the guy next door said "You'll never be able to build on it." But it was zoned Residential. There's a lot of wetlands. It's right on the creek. The neighbor said some other guy tried to build on it and it was denied.

By the Army Corps of Engineers?

Yeah. He said the guy lives right around the corner, you can go and talk to him. I went over and talked to the guy before I bought it and he says he just kept getting discouraged from the runaround and he just gave up. It was OK with me because it gave me a lot more bargaining power. I think they wanted like $16,000. So I went out and got the Army Corps of Engineers to delineate where the wetlands stopped on the property and I put flags on it on the side of the wetlands. The neighbor didn't like it too much because he had all private property without having to pay a nickel for it. But they didn't give me any trouble once I had it delineated.

So you felt comfortable doing what the other interested buyer couldn't do because you knew that you would build wherever you needed to. The other buyer might have wanted to build more in the center of the property. You said, "show me where the wetlands stop and I'll build around them."

You know, it was a little tricky building on it. I can remember right after I poured the slab, this giant monsoon hit. That was really weird. It was a freak event. It was like 9 inches of rain within a span of two hours. There was so much water on the slab and it was dumping off the side of my dirt and sloping down and eroding my land so I was just out there in the rain. I finally got it stabilized. I put in some retaining wall along there and put gutters on the house when I finally built the house so I wouldn't ever have that problem again. The water dumps right into the swamp.

Like I said, Billy doesn't see Wrenches as blocks in his life. It's a key to the way he lives that makes his life work. I am trying to learn that from him and think of this lesson daily. Imagine if the tropical storm hadn't happened until the house was completed. Billy may have lost the entire house. Since it occurred when he was in the process of building it, he was able to take a few days out, build a retaining wall and secure the home from monsoons and future hurricanes that may occur.

Billy, back to what you and Timmy did next. (Billy- Bill and Timmy -Tim are used interchangeably since everyone calls them both names.) So Timmy just kept working for the fitness center?

No, when we built the Arlington house, he quit the fitness center, too.

Tell me how you managed to live on 50% or less of your income throughout these years. How much do you live on in a year?

Less than $10 grand.

Does that include food and electric?

How I calculate that: My electric bill is almost nothing. This is a super-efficient house.

Looking at the giant single paned window/wall, I said, "Even with no double-paned window over there?"

These are 6 inch walls. The only windows that aren't doubles are there.

What's your electric bill?

Actually, since I built my electric car, it's gone up. It used to be $25/month. Now it's more like $35/month.

But you don't cook here?

Not now. I used to, but it never affected my electric bill. What affects my bills is when I do a lot of welding and stuff.

You do laundry here and use a dryer?

Un-huh.

But you don't have many clothes?

I have plenty of clothes.

Cook breakfast here?

No.

So you just contribute food to your Mom & Dad's and Patty's (sister's) house?

I cook more than half the meals over there. We only eat dinner together really. And my Mom does all the grocery shopping. Timmy does all the cleaning up, pretty much. We divide the grocery bills by the number of people.

I wondered if our Alaskan cousins, here on a long visit, were treated as part of the family: "Sheryl and Anna are cooking and sharing the cost of the food?

"Yes," replied Billy. "Sheryl and Anna are cooking once or twice a week."

You only eat one meal there? What do you do for breakfast?

I usually buy some cheese and tomatoes- or lettuce and turkey or lately, cereal.

You eat at your parent's home?

Yeah. I've been trying to lose some weight. I do eat breakfast out a couple of times a week on Wednesdays and Saturdays.

That's part of your $10,000 a year?

I don't really know how much I spend. The only thing I can do is take how many years I've been off and divide it by how much I sold my last house for.

But you think it's about $10,000/year or less.

It's changed since I bought my airplane. (Laughs.)

I thought you built your airplane from a kit so it didn't cost much.

I have a beautiful airplane out at the airport.

That's not the one you built from a kit. What happened to that one?

That one's downstairs, it's not a kit, it's a home-built plane. Some of them are kits. This is just an all-wooden airplane.

Does the one you built fly?

Yeah. But my other one's a lot nicer.

So your new one that you got is a regular factory-built airplane.

General aviation aircraft built in1966, cost $50 grand.

$50 grand! You paid cash for it?

Actually Timmy and I bought it together. Plan on using it when we go down to the Keys to fly up here to Jacksonville occasionally. It's a real fast airplane.

Me with Bill & Tim's Airplane
Madelyn Rubin

So, obviously splitting lots of big ticket items with Billy's brother, throughout the years, has made investments and fun things more affordable for him. They have a mutual interest to keep up on the maintenance of the particular vehicle or house, too.

*So, food you split with 4 or 5 family members. How much is **your** food a week?*
It costs me $300 bucks for 6 months for my share.

That's because y'all share the food. And cooking, is your part of that contribution too because somebody over there (at Parent's house) is handling all of the electric.

Right... this is insignificant. It doesn't take anything to cook.

You could have fooled me! That's always been a great rationale for me and my husband to eat out. "We're saving electricity!" Another myth I have to let go of.

Billy added, "Two things that cost you a lot in electricity: Central Heating & Air (HVAC), and the hot water heater. The rest of it is nothing."

But you take showers regularly. You use your hot water heater.

I built a solar hot water heater. Wintertime it doesn't do as good, but I have a hot water heater supplement.

Of course, I should have known. Billy is so analytical and frugal, that anything that costs the most, is what he will work on, decreasing his reliance on the expensive item and saving lots of money. "How much did it cost you to do that?" I asked.

That's the great part about hot water heaters. You know how much it cost me? It cost me the pipes to go up there and a couple of valves. Probably less than $20.

You've got it on the roof? But all of the materials! You've got the solar hot water panel to buy!

You can pick up all of the materials from the side of the road. The solar panel is just a piece of glass. Mine is an old glass door.

You didn't get a store-bought solar panel. Of course!

"Oh no!" Billy exclaimed. And a hot water heater you can pick up off the side of the road. They're all over the place! They're throwin' them out. If people could find something to do with them, they could help the garbage problem. There's no reason to throw them out. Usually it's an element or something that's gone bad. You don't need it for a solar water heater. You just need the tank.

You built your solar hot water heater.....the whole thing..... For $20?

Yeah. As a matter of fact, my parents have one now. Debbie (Billy's youngest sister) has one, Timmy has two. He uses one for his hot water and one for his dryer.

I guess if we paid y'all a couple hundred for doing a solar hot water heater for us… but you said several years ago that don't want to do stuff for relatives anymore.

It's not that we don't want to do stuff for relatives. We just don't want to do stuff.

Both of us laughed heartily.

"Cause you don't need the money," I said, a bit discouraged.

But, I could always give you the plans for it. You and Ned (my husband) could do it.

"Right!" I retorted, sarcastically. I have a bad neck. And Ned is an electronics guy among many other things, but when it comes to manual labor, he doesn't know what that means and doesn't want to learn what it means.

Nobody knows how to do it until… it's a matter of learning how to do it.

Ned is real good in electronics, though.

"That's all you need," Billy said making it sound extremely easy.

"Not quite," I reminded him. You need a person who is motivated to do manual labor. I have the motivation, but not the working body. Ned has the working body and the amazing mind, but not the motivation. We would probably just go and buy a panel to make it easier.

"It's a game changer when you install one" Billy said.

"They've got rules, too, with our homeowner's association," I added, continuing to pile on the objections.

Then I took a step back. Why would I be objecting to one of the most energy saving and money saving features that people can do for their homes and their wallets? Why wasn't I more receptive? Did I unconsciously want to help our local Jacksonville Electric Authority make more money, while draining our own financial resources? While I have purported for decades that energy efficiency is the best thing we can do for the earth and for ourselves, did I secretly want to help the rest of our population slowly destroy the earth?

"You're not allowed to have solar panels?" Billy asked.

Yeah, but we probably can't have ones that look like a door.

Did you look at mine? You can't tell it's a door.

Oh, you can't? I asked.

Uh-Uh!

Billy, you were saying that your Central Heating and Air, and your hot water heater, take up about...

Your solar hot water heater will take about 30% off of your total utility bill.

Our electric bill is about $300 a month. That's in the dead of winter and the dead heat of the summer. Otherwise, it's about $250. Have you heard of "Icynene® Insulation," the stuff they use to coat the ceiling of attics?

You gona spray that on there?" Billy asked.

"I don't know. Maybe" I replied.

There's a couple of good things that Icynene® does. It's a urethane foam that you spray on the ceiling of the attic.....it has some good points and some bad points. The good thing is it's a great insulator, great structurally. Also, seals out all the moisture. The only bad part that I've seen is the cost. Too, if you develop a roof leak, it's hard to see it since you have all that foam all over it. It's hard to see where the water is comin through.

I see. And they say you have to close off your roof vents too.

Right. That's the advantage.

"We have a programmable thermostat," I stated proudly. We let it go down to 71 at night, in the winter."

Billy's Solar Hot Water Heater in his Glass Door Solar Panel
Madelyn Rubin

Billy, responding non-judgmentally, replied, "A whole house fan is great. If you have a well-insulated home, like this one is, like in the summertime, you just turn on the fan and it pushes all that hot air out of the ceiling. I have mine on a timer. It only runs for an hour. Do the same thing in the winter time, wait till it gets up to a preset temperature then it moves all that hot air. You can always control what the temperature is in a house if you have a fan.

Yep. We would love your consultation. How much are you gona charge?

"You know what you could do without any effort at all? When do you take your showers?

I take mine in the morning.

Here's what you should do, Madelyn. This works, I've tested this and it's real easy. 10 minutes before you take a shower, turn on the hot water heater at the breaker. All it needs is 10 minutes to bring it up to temperature. If it's not hot enough in 10 minutes, give it 15 minutes. You have to test it a little bit. Turn it off before you take your shower. You can use the whole 40 gallons, cause it doesn't cost you a nickel more. Use everything in that tank. That way, your hot water heater only runs for 15 minutes a day. And Ned takes his at night, huh?

No, he takes one in the morning also.

So, you can leave it on. That's what I used to do in the wintertime when it was cloudy. I had a big ole hot water heater. It has more than enough hot water. That'll knock your bill down by 30%.

That would be great but I'd rather do a solar hot water heater. The cheapest we've heard a plumber install it for was $600.

That's a bargain.

That's a bargain? But YOU can do it for less than $200!

Laugh. That's a good deal! If he can put it in and buy it for you too?

No, I that was just for the labor.

"That's just for the plumbing, just for installation," Billy responded, knowingly.

Yeah, I think so. Not sure. I have to double check on it.

Oh. You better check on it with somebody else. I'd never make another one.

"Oh, really? Is it that hard?" I figured I'd caught him in his own web of frugalness this time.

Oh, no. It's just that you've got to get a hot water heater and everything. I mean, how much do you make in a day? What is your income?

You know, I'm on commission.

So am I, he said.

So far, this year, I've made about $40,000. But a lot of that now goes back to my business. I've got advertising and all this other crap.

Has this been a great year for you?

No, it's been an average year.

So, that's about $20 an hour, so an 8 hour day, $160 bucks. The solar hot water heater construction and installation takes 3 days maybe 4 days.

Not even worth getting the tools out. But I don't think you're gona get it done for $600.

"That's too hard a job then," I retorted.

No, it's not that hard. I just have more fun things to do. Laugh!

I don't blame you one bit. I do too! Laugh.

Billy went back to his original argument. "I mean, everybody's got the dexterity to be able to do it! If you can type on a typewriter, you have enough dexterity to build anything. The problem is if you can't lift something. That's where anybody can come into a problem.

"O.K." I said, giving up. Let me see what Ned (my husband) has to say about that.

I finally got it through my dense brain that Billy wasn't going to come over to our house to give me a consultation, no matter how much I paid him. If he did, that would start a domino effect with the other 100 cousins we have, who would want a consultation, too. And some of them would expect a free consultation. The bottom line for Billy: Freedom and free

Another Solar Hot Water Heater Installed by Billy at his Parents and Sister's Home
Madelyn Rubin

time are ALWAYS more valuable than money. If he saw his free time floating away from him, there is no way he would start doing energy efficient housing consultations. Most people have their price, if you want to buy their expertise. Billy expects you to do what he did. He'll even get you off to a good start by giving you some expert tips and telling you what you need. But don't try to take his free time away from him; doesn't matter what price you offer.

So, I went home and talked to my husband, Ned. After checking the cost of a professional Solar Hot Water Heater installation and the credits offered by the Feds, the State of Florida and the City of Jacksonville, we decided it was worth getting. We hesitated, knowing a new roof would be needed a few years down the road, but even figuring the cost of taking the solar panels down and reinstalling them (about $500) when the roof was replaced, it would STILL be worth doing. We knew we would be in the house another 5 years and that was the break-even point. *It didn't cost the $20 that Billy's solar hot water heater cost but we got it done. Our solar hot water heater and panel cost $2200 after we received the credits and rebates. Installed, it cost $3600.*

Back to my interview with Billy.

Billy, so I want to get back to how you manage on so little income. Your food bill is $300 for 6 months.

Yeah. Somewhere in there. I'd have to look it up. My Mom has a record.

Because there are 5 adults and 1 child that eat together on the average. You just share one of those meals a day. What do you do for lunch?

I just MAKE a meal for lunch. Like, I'll make a turkey sandwich or something.

That's all part of the $300 for 6 months?

Yeah. That's all part of the money. That's not bad, huh?

That's mind-boggling! Then you eat out, and clothes. What do you do about clothes?

The only thing I buy is socks and underwear.

And where do you get the rest of your clothes?

Friends. Everything I have is from friends.

They give them to you?

Yeah. More than I can use. More than I could ever wear. I have a hard time throwing them away until they get holes and stains. They last a lot longer.

If you saw Billy and you were his friend, you would want to give him clothes too. Summer or winter, he usually only has shorts and a t-shirt on.

33

You can tell these clothes have been worn many, many times. But it, obviously, doesn't bother Billy. You may think, ah hah! He doesn't have to buy work clothes. No wonder he gets by with so little money. If you haven't figured it out by now, if Billy had to get work clothes for a typical job, it would be no problem for him. Remember, he has had a few professional jobs and still lived on half his salary or less. If he had to, he'd have enough clothes within a week to take care of his entire wardrobe. He'd get them from garage sales, thrift shops or Goodwill. He'd know which friends to talk to who may have extra clothes around. He wouldn't spend over $10 for his entire professional wardrobe.

Wondering about the basics like toiletries, I asked, "And how about soap? Is that your soap that you use?" referring to the laundry soap he was making.

"No," Billy laughed. I get bar soap from Sam's. I use dishwashing detergent for shampoo. I found out it's the same thing as shampoo.

Cheaper than shampoo?

Oh, yeah. It's a lot cheaper.

Any particular dishwashing detergent you use?

Yep. As a matter of fact, there's an article on it in *Consumer Reports*. You can look it up in there. They'll tell you all about it; how it's a long-chain molecule and how it holds onto water on one side of the molecule, and holds onto dirt on the other side. That's what makes your hair clean. You rinse it out and it goes out with the water which holds the dirt.

Who cuts your hair?

I used to do it myself, but now Debbie (Billy's sister) does it. She uses clippers.

How often?

Every 5 months.

So, you've had it cut recently, about a month ago.

Actually, I let it go a little longer in the winter.

How about health insurance? Your Mom and Dad have health insurance?

They have Medicare. They're 80-something.

They had health insurance before that?

Yep.

You don't have health insurance. What if something terrible happened to you?

A long time ago, I accepted mortality.

No, no, I know you wouldn't need it if you were dead. But what if you don't die? What if you just need surgery?

I don't care. I decided how much I'm willing to spend my life [time] getting health insurance and it did not balance at all. I'm not willin' to get a job and work a 40 hour week. I'd rather die. It's just not worth it to me.

Yeah. But what if it was a simple surgery?

I'll never know, unless something happens. If I had cancer right now, I wouldn't know and I don't care to know.

You're three years younger than me, so you're 56. We'll both get Medicare. I've got about 6 years and you have 9.

I'll have some health insurance as soon as I get Medicare.

And glasses? You don't need glasses?

Yeah, I do. I wear glasses.

But those aren't regular glasses you got from an optometrist?

Oh, no, they're from the Dollar Store.

I laughed.

"Pretty good bargain," Billy said seriously. And you get all different weights too. Like when I'm welding, I have a much stronger one, but these are 1.00 or 1.25 Diopter or something.

Do you need glasses when you drive?

No, I need em when I fly.

You do? How come?

Hard to see the instruments. (Laugh) I can't back-up in the cockpit far enough. I can't fly from the back seat.

OK, so you can get those kinds of glasses that you need, but if you were terribly nearsighted, then you would need to get some prescription ones.

Oh, yeah. I've just been fortunate enough to have great health.

Hm…What else do you need… gas? That's all part of the $10,000?

Yeah. Well, actually I use my electric car.

Oh, where'd you get the electric car? Did you build it?

Um Hmm.

Was it a kit?

No! It's an old Volkswagen Rabbit Convertible.

It was a gas-powered car.

Yep, I took the gas engine out, bought this electric motor for it, bolted it onto the transmission, and put the batteries and voltage controller in it.

Hmm, I thought. Gives you a significant head start to be an engineer even if you can learn all of this online on the Internet. To Billy, "And how much did that cost you?"

Not a lot. The car itself cost $1500, the motor was like a $1000, the batteries were $70 bucks a piece and it required about 10 of them to start with. I've replaced them now, some of them.

How long do the batteries last?

These only lasted a year at most because they were the wrong kind. They were supposed to be a deep-cycle battery, they said they're a deep cycle, but the deep cycle ones keep a charge more. The new ones, you need twice as many of them, but they're the same price.

OK, so it was about $4000 to start with. The new batteries cost you an extra $800. And how long are these gona last you?

These will last a lot longer.

Two years?

Probably. I haven't even gotten rid of my old ones yet. I'm still using my old ones. So, it was $4000 for the car. So I don't need any gas. But if I need a car, Timmy has a truck and a car.

How far does this one go?

That one, when the batteries were new, I'd put about 12 miles a day on it.

And you plug it up at your home?

Unh-Huh.

If you wanted to go somewhere else, you didn't keep your other car?

No, I sold it to Jimmy [a nephew] and he sold it for twice as much.

Oh, really? I'll be darned. You got some money anyway. Did you know he was gona do that? Laugh.

Billy's Electric Volkswagen Convertible Rabbit
Madelyn Rubin

No, I gave him a good deal. But that's alright. I'm done with it.

"Uh, oh. He's a true member of the family!" I said.

No, well, I don't think it was sporty enough for him and he found one that was sportier.

So your biggest expense right now is food?

No.

What is it?

My airplane. That's right. I'm a half-owner and paid $25,000 for it. Aviation gas is like $5.00/gallon. It's the most efficient airplane you can buy. It gets like 20 MPG and it goes 180 MPH. It's pretty efficient.

Billy's Hand Built Electric Car
Madelyn Rubin

How long would it take y'all to go from the Keys to Jacksonville?

I've flown down there and it takes about 2 ½ hours.

Timmy has his pilot's license or just you?

Just me.

And y'all are gona take a car down there too?

Yep.

Which car?

We'll have the truck down there.

Timmy has a little bit bigger expense with his truck and gas.

39

"Yep," *Billy agreed.* Well, Timmy gets Social Security. Started getting it when his wife died. He has a **giant** income, a bigger income than he's ever had, which'll be what mine is if I can ever get 10 more quarters of social security employment.

You still need 10 quarters.

You need 40 total. 40 quarters is about 10 years. Looks good, having that income. I'd be livin' like a king.

Yep. You have how many years left to make 40 quarters before you turn 62? Two?

I have two and a half years left. Actually, you don't have to put in for the whole year.

You just have to put in a few months. You don't have to work full time?

 Right.

I say, "Do it"!

Well, I can just pay the social security into the system, probably without having to get an outside job. I just haven't done it yet. Keep putting it off. I've got a lot more years left before I need to get it.

Yeah, that's true, I chimed in.

Billy, back to your clothes. I am trying to cover all of the basics that people need and find out how you manage those things. If you ever need an overcoat or anything like that, somebody usually has one that fits you and gives it to you?

Oh, Yeah! Matter of fact, a friend of mine just gave me one that she found. I don't know how she got it, but she found it, thought of me, brought it home, put it through the laundry, it looks brand new. She brought it over for dinner one night, all wrapped up.

"Awwww," that's sweet, I laughed.

I'd wear it, but I've got a zillion coats.

"You don't ever go to Goodwill? I guess you don't need to," I said, now, realizing what Billy would say.

I don't need to. You know, I used to go in Atlanta sometimes when I'd go up to visit John, my oldest brother. Every Monday or Tuesday at the Atlanta secondhand store, they had a half-price sale, so for shorts, I'd get em for a buck.

You lived in Atlanta for a while, didn't you?

Just while we built a house up there. That was my last income, was that house that we built up there. "Okay, I'll tell you how much I paid," Billy said anticipating my next question.

What year was that?

Jessica was two, (she was born in 2000.) It was seven years ago, so that would be 2002, we sold the house. What happened is Timmy had a vacant lot up there right next to his house. His house was on two pieces of property. I was up there visiting one time and I said to Timmy, if you want to sell that lot, I want to buy it and build a house on it. He said, tell you what, let's build one [together] anyway. I'd already bought a piece of property down in the Keys for $62,000.

That's the one you're gona work on?

Yeah. His piece of property was worth like $60 grand or so. So, I traded him. We both ended up owning both pieces of property and we both built the house together right next door. That was my last income and it cost, that house was a little expensive to build, it was like $50 grand to build.

You had to go higher because it was a higher-end neighborhood.

Well, yeah. I also built another house in Atlanta- Patty's.

Yeah. I remember that one.

So that's… subtract out $50 grand for the materials and another $60 grand for the plot after real estate expenses. We had a REALTOR® do that one. Probably closer to $320,000. $110,000 for the expenses, from $320. $210,000 divided by two. That's $105 grand each. It took a year to build it, but I've been livin off of it for 7 years and have some in the bank still. Tells you how much I've spent.

What do you do with that money now? Do you invest?

Now I invest.

Do you invest in stocks?

Yep.

Now how do you pick your stocks?

Wrote a little program for choosing my stocks. You know, I did the worst thing. What happened was I decided to get into stocks in 1999. As soon as I got into it, we had the first dot.com bubble burst. So all my stocks went down in value. But, I brought them all back up. I have always done better than the S & P 500 or the Dow Jones industrial.

Awesome.

Got it up to a really pretty good amount. Since 1999, I've had a hundred and eighteen thousand dollars in there of my own money.

So you made…….

No, I didn't make anything. This last recession killed me again! Up until last November, until we got our new president by coincidence, the market was terrible! I lost my ass again!

But you don't have everything in it!

No. I have a lot of property.

But you still don't have all your savings in it? Maybe half?

No. I've got everything....everything I have extra is in the stock market, that's not in property.

"Ooooooh," I said fearfully, remembering a book I read in the 1980's that you should always diversify your money. That way if one investment goes south, you have the others to fall back on. Of course, I forgot that since then, the experts are saying that for the first time in the U.S. economy, everything is going south at the same time. It doesn't matter where you put your money.

"It's doin great!" Billy said enthusiastically. What happened was: let's say I had $118,000 in it basically and last November [almost] everything I had was lost. It went down to like $59,000 but I was still doin better than everybody else. And NOW it's up to like $140,000.

Cause you're choosing your own stocks.

If you think about it from November till now, it's 130% return.

That's awesome!

So, I think it's a good vehicle, if you don't have idiots in there NOT regulating Wall Street.

Wall Street's still skimmin' and scammin' like crazy?

Yeah. Right. But, I'm gradually getting better.

"Yeah, I can imagine. So you are your own stock broker, so to speak," I said thinking how much my cousin, Billy, has effectively gotten five Masters Degrees by learning on his own in our U.S. libraries and now on the Internet.

"Yep," said Billy in his matter of fact way. I buy through Scottrade®... $7 a trade. It's doin good.

"So you're helping all your relatives?" I asked, still hoping I wouldn't have to study the disgusting stock trade market for years.

Actually, Patty [Billy's sister] and my Mom, we all have the same account.

Who makes the choices? Do you?

Um hm. I have the lion's share of it. In the past, Mom had a mutual fund, something called the GrinKo fund, or something like that. She always called it her Shrinko fund.

We both laughed.

Mom was so mad. She was waiting for it to recover, you know. She started out with 5 grand, and it went down. Finally it recovered and got back up to $2500. You might get your money back if you keep it there, you might not lose any money, but you're missing all the opportunities of it growin more with a decent stock. So, finally she gave me that money and we put it in there.

I replied in my normal, ignorant fashion regarding investments: "Now, falling twice like you have Billy, I'm surprised you're not skimming some off the top for a safe vehicle like CDs."

"Safe?" said Billy, chagrined. "I think CDs are like cash really. Cash is a terrible investment."

"Just kind of as a backup?" I said.

I don't need it, you know.

"Oh, so you do keep cash?" I asked.

I have enough to live off of. Like I just looked at my bank account yesterday and I've got $3000.

You have enough for 6 months or so? Probably sell something if you needed to?

44

"You know," Billy said, thoughtfully, his mental wheels spinning, "actually it's not my airplane that really costs me, its property taxes. Those are the killers, man. Those things'll eat the hell out of ya."

"Especially with riverfront property," I chimed in.

Yeah, well, I have 4 different properties.

Then my mind lit up with the thought of The Big Kahuna. "Oh, the property in the Keys."

I got those 3 lots over there on the water, got this property. This property's probably similar to the Keys, valued at $110000. I also have 20 acres on a lake in Palatka, Florida.

So how about your lots in the Keys?

Well, we have two pieces of property down there. We own one with Lisa [my brother's daughter] in Ramrod Key.

Oh, really!

Lisa, Patty, Timmy and I have one piece of property.

Is that the one y'all are gona build on?

No. The other one. The other one's further away. It's on Marathon Key on Sombrero Road.

And keep em? For vacation?

Uh huh.

As you see, Billy is not always forthcoming with information. While he agreed to talk to me, he didn't say he would easily let the words spill out.

The Second Interview - 2010

Billy, how did you get the values that you did? How were you raised? Sometimes people obtain their values by emulating what their parents did and sometimes they get their values by doing the opposite. They change them because they don't like certain things.

"Yep" Billy said as a matter of fact, "I think you're right, Madelyn. I guess my conservatism…**fiscal** conservatism…comes from when we were young, we were always worried about makin it to the next month, just like, I'm sure, many families were. It wasn't anything special, but I kinda took it to heart. It was nice at the end of the month if we'd get to go to Burger King for dinner."

"As far as my freedom issues, that was probably generated by my Dad. He believed that 'life is 98% work and 2% pleasure.' Never made any sense to me and I didn't want any part of that."

I didn't have to ask Billy about his work ethic. I know where that came from. Since Billy's Dad, Uncle George, came from the same family as my Mom, I know what he had been taught. Our grandparents, having raised our parents on the farm in Lake Butler, Florida, needed the kids to work from dawn to dusk to put food on the table and keep the house and the out buildings repaired. The kids needed to help tend the animals and tend the gardens. It was critical for the family's survival. Uncle George, being a school teacher, and having 5 kids, he couldn't stray far from that ethic, even though his wife always worked as a nurse.

It seems somehow, in America, we have continued the pattern of working from dawn till dusk, while many of us really haven't had to. But most of us did not come to the conclusion that Billy did or, at least, we didn't know how to change things. So we got into a pattern of working long hours, buying things on credit and doing what Wall Street, Madison Avenue, and the media said was a good thing to do. As long as we stay in debt, even mortgage debt, we are stuck in a pattern of always trying to keep up and never quite making it. Thus, we are always borrowing more money to make ends meet, or to get that new item that everyone else already has.

Billy & Tim at Bill's Jacksonville home
Madelyn Rubin

With the way technology advances daily, that means a new television, computer, cell phone, IPad, and more "new" every month; that is, if we want to keep up. And who doesn't? Billy sees the pattern. He has decided that he doesn't want to follow the masses. He sees the freedom of these people lost and their happiness lost with it.

Back to questions for Billy:
You were gona prove to your Dad that it didn't have to be that way?

No, I didn't have anything to prove to him. I just didn't want to be like that, you know. I guess the two things that are the most prominent in my values are:

1. Education, not necessarily formal, but I'm not against formal, and
2. Freedom.

I think that was probably instilled into me by that 98% work ethic that my Dad used to preach. Not necessarily what his example was [he laughs], but I guess that's what he tried to instill in us.

So were y'all pushed to work a lot when y'all were kids and not play? You didn't have time to play much?

Oh, no, we didn't do much playing. We just kinda dreaded it when my Dad came home.

He would always have chores for y'all to do?

Like Saturday mornings, we'd try to be REAL quiet. We didn't want to wake him up. The longer he could sleep, the better it was. Maybe that's where my "get up early" ethic is. We all got up early and we had all our freedom then, before mom and dad got up.

So your mom was with him on all that. What did she say?

She didn't see anything wrong with it.

And you said when you were younger, you'd have to live month-to-month like a lot of families do. But, looking from the outside, your family has always seemed pretty frugal. Why do you think they had to live month-to-month, other than having 5 kids and 2 people working with middle-class incomes?

That was a lot more so, in the early years than the later years. Like when we lived up here in Jacksonville [in the early '60's], my Mom's was the only income. My Dad was struggling to get through college. Then he taught at Fletcher High School for a couple of years, I guess. I'm not sure for how long. He would take on extra loads just to get enough money to make it by.

How old were you when you lived in Jacksonville initially?

I guess we moved down to Miami when I was in third grade, from Jacksonville. Grew up in Miami. When we lived in Jacksonville, Dad would take my Mom to work, the late shift, 11pm to 7am. He'd drive her from the beach and drop her off at St Vincent's Hospital and come back, because she didn't drive back then. We were required to stay awake while he took her to work. We were usually up till he got back. We were on "Fire Duty." He'd leave four kids at home all by themselves, you know, while he took my Mom to work. It was kinda rough, trying to stay awake.

What do you mean "Fire Duty" I asked curious, since I had never heard of the term from any family members. You know how word gets around in families.

You'd get your ass kicked if you fell asleep. If there was a fire, we could all run outside. I was in third grade, John (oldest brother) was in 7th grade, and Patty was in 4th grade. My Dad wanted to make sure that if anything happened, we were awake.

How long did that go on?

I guess, until we moved to Miami.

About 3 years?

But then we moved to Miami. It was kinda funny. My Dad rented this U-Haul truck. We all got in the cab, all seven of us in the U Haul truck. It was tight. John had to lay across the seat in the back the whole way from Jacksonville to Miami. Mom had two kids, one on each knee. I was closest to my Dad, shifting gears. As a matter of fact, my Dad pulled off to take a nap after the previous day loading the truck. He was worn out. The police stopped to give him a ticket for parking on the side of the road. Then [the cop] realized that my Dad had his hands full already, so he just let him go. Then we make it to Miami and they went out and bought a car. I can't remember how it happened, but I know that this car got repossessed, because of a Shell Oil debt. He had a credit card with Shell Oil, you buy gas with that, he got behind on his payments and the car got repossessed. He was catching rides to work for a while.

Is that what brought you all down to Miami, your Dad's work?

Yeah.

What kind of work was that?

He worked for Miami Dade Community College.

So, he went from teaching high school to community college, where the pay would be a little bit better.

Right.

And your Mom worked in Miami too, right?

Yeah. Like I said, by normal standards we were poor. Rich enough to have things, but poor enough to get your car repossessed.

I wonder, Billy, if the gas thing must have been connected to the car, or that's just how you remember it as a kid and maybe it was separate? You said your dad couldn't pay for his gas card.

"My Mom said Shell Oil Company repossessed the car," Billy replied confidently. "Now, I'm sure that in order to get credit, he had to put his car down as collateral."

It finally hit me. The early stages of what became the ruinous Home Equity line. But this was a "Car Equity line." Amazing! "Oh, I see," I said as the light went on. "Oh, my goodness. How terrible. Those were some tough times, weren't they?"

"Not compared to what your grandparents had to deal with, I'm sure," Billy replied.

My grandparents didn't have such a tough time, either side.

I thought your Mom had a tough time.

She did, after both her parents died. That's when it was tough. Otherwise, it wasn't too tough for her.

Yeah, my Mom only remembers happy times from her childhood. They always had plenty to eat. And having a grocery store, that helped. And Grandma knew how to take advantage of things that were getting ready to expire at the grocery store. Mom says that they always had fresh vegetables that were getting ready to go bad.

Plenty to eat, some good times, Christmas and so on. So y'all were in Miami for 10, 15 years?

Let's see, I was eight years old, third grade when I arrived. Went my first two years of college at the community college my Dad taught at, 'cause we got free education there.

John and Patty did too?

Yeah. Patty did. John would go to college on and off. He would sign up for courses and not go to them. He didn't get a two year degree down there.

So after your two years of college, y'all moved back up here to Jacksonville.

No, the family were still down there. I came up to the University of Florida in Gainesville after I finished school in Miami. Patty and I rented a camper trailer lot for college.

So in terms of your childhood, you saw that it was difficult and you didn't want to live month-to-month. When did you decide that; how old would you say you were?

There was no physical timeline for deciding. I was just brought up to be frugal. I probably pretty much have always been that way.

Your family was frugal, right?

I don't know.

Do you think that's why you never had kids...never had a family because you didn't want it to be so hard?

No, no, I don't think it'd be difficult to have kids.

Financially?

No, I see kids as not costing much more than being by yourself. You have the same housing expenses. Kids don't eat as much as adults do 'till they get to be teenagers, I guess. Education's pretty much paid for by the state.

You've got medical care.

Well, I don't use medical care. It's a waste of money. There's no value, I should say.

Some people grow up like you did and they say "I'm going to make so much money, I'll never be in that situation again." You didn't make that decision. You said, "I'm gona be so frugal...

...that I won't need money. It seems like in the way you propose it, there's no limit to how much you actually need, and you can keep goin and goin and goin. You make a million, you need 2 million, and then you need 100 million.

That's what many people do.

I never wanted that track...never needed that track.

How did you know what would need to happen for you not to be in the situation that your family was in, and so many other families are in?

They never had a nickel in the bank. They were always in debt. I've rarely been in debt. So, I figure, "if you're not in debt, you don't need a job."

So that was the main thing: <u>to not be in debt.</u>

Right.

And you don't remember when you decided that? Did you decide when you were 10, 20, 25 years old?

It had to have been pretty young to come up with that realization. I know like when I was 18, my first vehicle was a motorcycle. I had to go into debt to buy it. I didn't like the feeling of it right away and paid for it in 3 months.

Cause it reminded you of your childhood?

I just don't like being in debt. It takes your independence ...it takes your freedom when you're in debt. You're no longer free. You're indentured.

Like your Mom and Dad were. Because they were in debt all the time.

Right.

Indentured by the credit card (I call them "Debtor's Cards") from the pushers on Wall Street.

We both Laughed.

"Actually, since I'm a Wall Street stockholder I can't protest too much!"

So here it is. A core value of Billy's: **"If you're in debt, you lose your freedom; you lose your independence."** *Isn't freedom and independence what America stands for? How did most of us fall into this debt trap and lose both freedom and independence?*

Back to Billy…

So those are the values that helped you decide you definitely didn't want to be in debt. Did everybody else in your family make the same decision?

I would say there's a common theme here. I don't know if any of them are as extreme as I am.

How would you say you're more extreme than your siblings?

They're all willing to go and get jobs and go to work for The Man. Patty, she's pretty frugal. She makes a decent income, but she never wants for anything, never cares about making more than she makes already.

So you help her invest her money. She could probably quit work if she wanted to?

Oh, yeah. She probably could. But, she enjoys her job. I think that's kind of the key to life…if you enjoy your job **and** have your freedom. Debbie works for the JEA. She enjoys her job. She doesn't need nearly as much money as they pay her. She even tells them that, and that she would rather not have to work overtime. If she could work 20 hours a week, she'd go for that, I'm sure. As a matter of fact, she's working 7 days a week right now for an outage at the JEA.

Does she eat meals with y'all sometimes?

Rarely.

So now that Debbie has moved down the street from your parents, everybody lives within a two-mile radius from them, except for John.

Tim, Billy's Brother and Business Partner
Madelyn Rubin

So you guys are heading to the Keys and building there . What are the lots going for now?

David, your nephew, bid $70,000 on a lot. Thought it was a great price. On a canal; ocean access within 300 yards.

So now in Jacksonville, everyone (almost) lives within a two-mile radius of each other.   Even though your Dad worked you really hard, when y'all were kids, there seems to be a strong, strong bond.

Yeah. It was us against the parents.

Bench built by Tim in Billy's home
Madelyn Rubin

Wait a minute, if that were the case, everybody wouldn't live so close to your parents now.

No, not necessarily. Once you become an adult, there's a different pecking order. You're not the lowly person on the Totem Pole when you're an adult.

So your Dad doesn't try to tell you what to do anymore.

Oh, he could try, but it doesn't work.

Does he try still?

No. We wouldn't listen to him.

Y'all are there to take care of them and help them out and there's a lot of kids that live miles and miles and miles away and never get close.

Yep. Patty lives right up above them.

So what do you think was the main thing that made y'all do that...that you live so close to your parents?

Well, my parents lived way out in Northside, so I probably lived 20 miles away from them. Then, Patty wanted to move down. She was getting sick of Atlanta. She wanted to move down here and they wanted waterfront property. I have creek front, so there's a good chance that no matter where they moved, it could be close to here. They found about 3 or 4 places, all relatively close to here. The one they got is on the water. Then Timmy, he lost his wife, and wanted to have someplace close to Grandma and Patty so he could have help taking care of Jessica. He moved into the same neighborhood. Debbie happened to see a house that was for sale in the same neighborhood. It was a good deal, so she bought it. That's how we all ended up here, I guess. So, for 20 years they lived out there in Northside and we weren't all that close together. So, it's just, more or less, a coincidence, I think.

I chuckled. Having been a practicing family therapist off and on for two decades I know it's rarely 'a coincidence.' I said that to Billy, using my best, matter of fact therapeutic voice.

You know, now it's convenient 'cause we all have to eat three times a day. Typical American, you have to eat at least three times a day. We don't have that much tendency to be malnourished, so for me to cook over here, them to cook over there, and Timmy to cook where he is...it's convenient for us all to meet for meals, because it's not that far away. And it gives me the opportunity to win a few quarters off my Mom.

How's that?

We play Gin and Showdown and 31.

At each meal? Cool!

Matter of fact, she took 50 cents off me today.

Oh, darn! What do y'all play for, nickels or quarters?

Quarters.

Speaking of your family being close, I know that your role with Jessica, when Timmy first came back to Jacksonville with her, was really, the role of a mother, to an extent. I don't know who else did that, but I know you did. You'd get her up in the morning, help her get ready for the day. Do you still play that role?

She likes brushing her hair, herself now. Course, I taught her how to do it," Billy said proudly. She used to be a mess! [Voiced softened, lovingly]. Now, she's pretty much neat every day. She has her hair all tied back in a ponytail. She brushes her hair. It used to be a pain in the neck to get her to do it. You know, it'd get so tangled. She'd wait too long. I'd have to get all the knots out for her. But she likes doin it herself.

Who gets her up in the morning now and makes sure she gets breakfast, and makes sure she gets to school on time and all that?

It could be anybody in the family. Usually, Timmy or myself.

I asked her the other day whom she spent time in the evening with, most of the time. She said, "I watch movies sometimes; I'm with Uncle Bill usually watching movies. When Dad goes to bed, I go to bed." So Dad (Timmy) must be there, too?

Yeah, Bill replied. If Timmy's next to the TV, he's fallin' asleep. (A family trait that I have also inherited.) So, if there's a movie to watch, Jessica and I watch it. Especially if it's scary, because she doesn't like watchin scary things by herself. But when I say scary, it's not necessarily scary. It's like a mystery. Not a horror movie.

In terms of shopping for her clothes, who does that with her?

Aunt Patty takes her shopping quite a bit. I don't ever take her shopping. Sometimes Debbie does. My Mom will usually do her laundry for her.

Rarely does Timmy take her shopping; Timmy and I feel the same about shopping. Kind of boring. It's just not our thing.

Don't want to spend the money?

No. We spend plenty of money, as it is.

Maybe it's a girl thing. Everybody helps with Jessica. Everybody chips in.

"Right. It's not a chore, though," Billy replied.

Speaking of chores, does Jessica have chores at home?

Sometimes. Her chore is to keep that dining room floor swept up. She's supposed to keep her room clean.

But it's Timmy's room too.

Right. But her part is supposed to be clean.

So, how are y'all going to manage when y'all go to the Keys by boat? Where's the sailboat?

It's in the back of my parents' house.

And you can sail from back there because it's on the river?

Uh huh.

That's where y'all are gona start.

Yeah. We already brought it up from Ft Lauderdale to right there.

And that's a $50,000 boat, you said?

Oh, no, no, no. My airplane was $50,000.

That's a...$20,000 boat?

We bought it for $8,000.

Because it needed work?

It needed **total** rework. But it'll be a very expensive boat when we get finished with it.

A $30,000 boat?

Maybe.

And how many feet is it?

32 or 34.

How many people does it sleep?

It'll sleep…There's a bunk. If you're in there with your wife it could sleep more, but just unfamiliar people, it could sleep 1, 2, 3, or 4.

It's got a place to eat and a toilet?

Uh huh. Well, it doesn't have any of that stuff yet. We're working on it.

Did it have it at one time?

Yeah. It did. I'll show you pictures of it sometime. How bad it was. It was so bad that we took the boat from Ft. Lauderdale up to here and we wouldn't even go inside.

Oooooo. Was it worth $8,000? I guess so. Y'all got a good deal?

I guess so. If you're tryin to build it from scratch, it'd be worth a lot more than that.

So are y'all gona teach Jessica how to sail?

Oh yeah! She's gona know how to sail, know how to fish. I already told her that the Jon boat that I just built is hers. Might even have to drive it to school, I told her.
[Laughing.] Just kidding.

You bought her a Jon boat?

We had a Jon boat already. Gona use it as a tender. I cut it in half so that it'll fold over inside itself. So you can set it on the back of the sailboat. When we need a tender you can unfold it.

What's a Tender?

A Tender boat is like a small rowboat that you use to get to service the big boat and to go ashore.

I see. So, where did you learn how to sail?

Out of a book. Everything's in the library or online now. You know, it used to be, I'd spend a lot of time in the libraries. But now you can find it so much quicker online.

Billy & Tim's Boat
Madelyn Rubin

So you learned to sail when you were pretty young? 25, 30?

No. When you say, "learned to sail," I mean that's assuming that I know how to sail now.

Does that mean you know how to sail?

Yeah.

So when did you go out on your first sailing trip?

My first sailboat was a little Sunfish. Do you know what a Sunfish is?

No.

It's probably like a 14 foot fiberglass-formed boat. There isn't really an inside to it at all. It's like you kind of sit on the surface of it and my friend and I, we found it sunk in this lake. Picked it up, took it back and my friend, Gerald, and I and his dad restored it. His father did all these drawings for me (Billy shows me nice drawings on the walls of his home.) We grew up together.

Sample of Sunfish Sailboats

How old were you when you got that boat?

We got that when I was 16 or 17.

You were 16 or 17! So this was down in Miami.

Umm hummm.

So that's your first sailing experience.

Actually, no. That's my second sailing experience. Our first one was when John and I built this Kayak sailboat out of wood and canvas. It was kind of a disaster. We built this boat. We had no idea how to build a boat. But we put it together. We bought this canvas from Sears, Roebuck. It's this cotton duck cloth and we wrapped it around the structure that we built, we cobbled together and then we sprayed it with this waterproofing to keep the water out. We launched it; it sinks right to the bottom.

[Both laugh.]

Now, let me ask you a question. You must have been about 14, right?

Yeah. We couldn't drive then.

When you were doing that, since you were working on something, then your Dad didn't bother you, right?

"Uh, I don't know," Bill replied in a very puzzled voice. "He didn't have any objections to us doing that, no."

*So as long as y'all were busy doing **something**, he didn't complain.*

Oh, no. If it interfered with what he wanted done, it took second place. You didn't get away with…

Trying to do something for yourself?

Yep, but, you know, as we got older, we got more freedom.

Oh, you did! Good.

So, I'd say, by the time we were 16 or so, I mean, we **all** had to stand up to him sooner or later 'cause that's how you know you made it.

So, back to the boat. That one sunk, so did y'all just leave it there?

Oh, no! We picked it up, took it back to the house, got some house paint my Dad had left over down in the basement….just cans of paint…and painted it all over with 3 or 4 coats of house paint. Took it back out there, floated great!

"Really!" I said in a surprised voice. "Wow!"

But it never did sail that well cause it was pretty tippy, you know. That was our first sailing experience.
That's pretty impressive!

It was pretty ugly… but it worked.

Yeah, it worked! Cool. Then you had the Sunfish boat. How do you stay on that thing if they're just flat?

It has a cockpit and it's about this big...about 2 feet by 2 feet. But you sit on the surface of it.

What keeps you from just falling right off into the water?

You can fall off. We fell off many a times. If the Boom swings, it can knock you off too.

So y'all have graduated. This new one is a big timer here. It's the biggest boat y'all have had? 32 feet?

Yeah.

So y'all are gona teach Jessica how to sail and I guess, you'll be cooking.

We'll be working on the house plan while we sail.

How are you gona eat?

We've never had a problem finding some way to eat. [Laughs]

I mean, y'all gona be cooking on the boat or what?

Yeah. That'll be our galley.

So it'll have a little refrigerator and stuff?

It'll have a refrigerator, microwave.

And y'all will be fishing?

Yep.

Y'all fish out there off your Mom & Dad's dock?

No. Jessica did. She enjoyed it.

She get something?

Something bit her line, but she didn't get it in.

Do y'all have to watch out for 'gators out there?

I think there are a few gators out there, but I've never seen one. I've seen otters and turtles.

So, y'all are gona be sailing off in August, 2010.

That's the plan. Things can change, depending on when we get our permit in the Keys. We should have our permit by then.

Is Jessica excited about it?

I think so.

How about schooling? What kind of schooling are y'all gona do for her?

She'll be down there going to school.

Oh. You're not going to do home schooling.

Nope. She'll be off to school every day.

You don't want her to help all day every day. She's in the 4th grade?

She's nine years old.

Does she ask much about her Mother?

Uh, sometimes. Not that often anymore.

Got pictures of her mother?

Yeah. She doesn't really remember her.

On to a less painful subject: I don't want you to tell me your whole program about stocks, because that's a personal thing that you may not want everybody to know about, but I'm just wondering if you can tell me something about how you choose your stocks without giving away your trade secrets.

I'll tell you exactly how I do it. I have, like, 9 stock indicators that I like to monitor. I try to pattern a company after how I would run it, conservatively. So, a stock that has low debt ranks high with me. A stock that has a current ratio....current is the amount of assets to deficits....a lot more assets than it has debt...that's very valuable to me. What else, oh, it's margins. What kind of return it has on equity, 4 different margins that it has; how much earnings it has, its price-to-earnings ratio, price-to-sales, and price-to-book value. I send them all through this equation and it'll give me a number and I have a cutoff as to where I will purchase the stock. When it comes out of the equation, if it's less than 25, I consider it a valuable company. If it's more than 25, I consider it's got too much on the bad side. That's how I determine if the stock is what I want. Now the second question is when to buy it and when to sell it. If the price of the stock is too high relative to its earnings, then I won't buy it. If it's real low relative to its earnings, then I will buy it. And when you look at its historic earnings, if it becomes nearer to where its historic earnings are, I mean, that's a line where I'll sell it too. I'll buy it low relative to earnings and sell it once is gets high relative to its earnings.

So what do you think about the machines they have out that do the superfast trading?

Fast trading doesn't matter to us. They're trading on 1/10%. Their advantage is that they have billions of dollars and fancy equipment. We are low-profile bottom feeders. I created a program 3 years ago. It did great until the stock market crashed. I stuck to the same program and am in the lead again. I used Excel® to create the program. There's an equation anybody can work out for themselves. I like a company that doesn't have a lot of debt, because it is safer. Someone else may want to take the risk of betting on companies that have a higher debt-to-equity ratio. The equation analysis is for safety mainly, but not exclusively. I look at value, too.

So you do this daily or weekly?

No, you only need to do it like once a month.

Once a month is when you look at it?

It doesn't mean I don't look at it more often. I look at it for curiosity's sake all the time. I don't have to do anything with it. But if you do look at it regularly, it gives you some insights and if something happens weird on a stock, you'll catch it before it gets too far away from you. So you really only have to do it once a month, 'cause once a month, all your "sells" and your "buys" expire. Before I ever buy a stock, I know what I want to sell it for. And the day I buy it, I'll put a sell in on it too. Unless there's too giant a gap, then the brokerage firm won't let you. Like if you buy a stock for $10 and you want to sell it for $35, there's too big of a gap there and the brokerage firm won't take the sell.

So a $10 difference is all they'll do?

It depends. If it costs $500 a stock, $10 is relatively small and they'll take the sell order.

So you don't mind me publishing your method? That is __very__ interesting! You've done all this in an equation.

What Billy bases his equation on:

Nine Stock Indicators:

1. Debt-to-Equity	6. Price-to-Sales
2. Price-to-Earnings	7. Price-to-Book
3. Current Ratio	8. Return on Assets
4. Return on Equity	9. Profit Margin
5. Operating Margin	

Billy continues:
"I started out, you know, going to the library and looking all this stuff up and that was a royal pain. I'd spend a lot of time over at Jacksonville University going through…they have these giant catalogs, they're business catalogs…there's a certain company that puts them out and gives all the specs on all the companies. Now you can get them online at the touch of a button. Makes it a heck of a lot easier. You don't have to spend nearly as much time."

That was valuable time that you spent in the libraries all those years because it taught you how to research.

Yeah. Sure did! And I always loved going to the library. There's something really cool about a library, I think. I believe, that if today's kids spent more time in the library and less time watching sports (or playing certain video games), they'd be a lot better off.

Me too. You are truly a self-made man! You have taught yourself so much!

You know, I like education. It's formal and informal.

And who impressed education upon you? Was it your parents that did that?

68

Uh, no, I don't think so. I've always liked building things and making things. You can find out that somebody did it before you and you're that much further along. That's why I always liked going to a library.

And if you do it yourself, you won't be in debt.

Right. Yeah, and if you know how everything works, you're not afraid of things. Like, I'm not afraid of a hurricane coming in here and tearing down my house, because I know I can build it back. So I don't care about insurance. It means nothing to me. I can take a chance just as good as they can. I can be a lot more efficient at taking the chance.

By the way, how thick did you say the walls of this home are? 6 inches?

6 inches.

So you did 2 X 6 framing?

2 X 6 studs. It's really not the wall. The wall is thicker than that.

R 30 insulation in the walls?

No. R 19. R 30 in the ceiling.

By the way, Billy, we decided to get a solar heater.

Oh, good!

A little bit more than $800. There are 3 different incentives right now. Even with all those incentives, we still could only get it down to $3600 quite a ways from $800. But we got a 40 gallon panel for the roof. Then we got a new 40 gallon HWH because the one we have now is older, a 1996.

That's cool. You'll see a difference in your electric bill.

And they said that it covers 80% of your hot water.

Did they say what the payback is gona be?

About 3 years. The secret is keeping your house after you've done all that [spoken like a true REALTOR®. who usually buy and sell their homes often.] Except the newer homes are a lot better insulated.

You'd know better than anybody. Does a solar water heater add to the value of your house?

Yeah. If you say up front, when you're selling it, that a solar water heater saves $90 bucks a month, that will help.

Yeah. You ought to keep your before and after bills so that you can show people, if you decide to sell. That way you recover value when you decide to sell it. It won't matter that much if you sell it early. That's probably the simplest thing you can do for helping your energy situation.

I was thinking of doing that Icynene® Insulation, too. I haven't checked the price yet.

How much was your credit for the solar?

$800 from the electric company, JEA; $500 from the State of Florida and 30% of the total, after the $800 credit, from the Federal government as a tax credit. [Note: the state of Florida reduced the rebate to $200 and we received it almost three years after installation.] Our upfront costs were $3600, not $20 like yours was, Billy.

So Billy, what are you the most proud of, in all of the things that you've done?

I guess, freedom. Yeah.

Financial freedom?

It's having the freedom to know that I don't have to be somewhere. It's nice to know that I can do whatever I want, any day I want to. I have a boat down there. But I've got the freedom to go whenever I want.

But the thing is, you don't want extravagant things and that's why you can live the way that you live. In other words, what if you wanted to travel?

It wouldn't be expensive for me to travel.

To go to Europe every couple of years?

I don't know. People think that I have extravagant things now. I have a very expensive airplane, boats…

Those costs were shared with Timmy. Who in the hell thinks you're extravagant? I'd like to meet them!

We both laugh.

You don't think I'm a little bit extravagant?

No! Not even close. I think you're eccentric, not extravagant.

Well, you know, I don't think it would cost me a lot to travel, if I wanted to go to Europe. I've gone to Belize and it didn't cost me much. The most it cost me was getting there cause, once there, I don't like goin' to the touristy areas of anyplace I go. I want to go see the culture. And when I went down there, the same trip [total cost] that cost me $500, costs a typical American $2500.

But where did you stay and where did you eat?

I stayed at cheap hotels and went to the local eateries. I went to the Dominican Republic one time and it was one of my worst trips, except for the company I kept. I went there with my brother, John, and two of his buddies. We stayed in this resort. It was just like the United States, like a fancy resort in the US. We didn't experience <u>any</u> of the Dominican Republic's culture, really. The only part we saw was when we rode a bus from the airport to this resort. They wanted to make sure you didn't get off anywhere. But you drive in the bus and you look outside and you see that it didn't look anything like this resort did. If you want to travel in fancy resorts, it <u>is</u> going to cost you a lot of money.

And you don't get to see much.

And you'll just be basically in the United States (He he!) But you know, your brother, Lou, he's got a pretty cheap way of traveling.

That's cool, isn't it? It's called Friendship Force. (Find out more about *Friendship Force International* at www.friendshipforce.org)

I don't think it costs him that much.

It can get pretty costly, even the way that he does it with his travel group. But it's a great group.

"I admire the way he does that," Billy said.

Oh, I do, too! It's not cheap because they eat at a lot of restaurants and go to a lot of places and stuff. But I love that they stay at local people's houses in different countries, you know? That's really cool! Perfect for him!

Wouldn't be perfect for you, though, huh?

My husband: He's graduated considerably from what he used to do. He used to be married to a woman whose parents were quite wealthy, so they always lived very extravagantly, particularly when they travelled because her parents would pay many of the travel bills. They always travelled First Class, went to the most expensive hotels, and ate at the most expensive restaurants.

"How'd they get their millions?" Billy asked.

I don't know a whole lot of the details regarding how they made their money. I think it was mainly through clever real estate investments and inherited money. Real estate was a good way to make it. I used to think that real estate was the best investment ever. I still think it's a great investment, but today the carrying costs can kill ya.

And the buying it and getting rid of it can kill ya. Whereas, stocks, you can trade $10,000 worth of stocks for $7.

"As long as you know what you're doing" I added.

And you don't have to contact anybody. You can just do it with the push of a button! So, I've kind of changed. For my primary real estate holdings, I always believed in buying waterfront. I still do, but it can be very expensive to hold onto, with the state on your butt the whole time for taxes.

To diversify is always good. Y'all don't have any rental properties. Rentals take a toll on you quick!

Patty has one—a rental. It's a condominium.

She has to pay monthly fees. I don't like that.

Yeah. I don't either. I don't think she has a mortgage on it.

Oh, she's paid it off?

Yeah. She bought a piece of waterfront property out there in Ponte Vedra, FL. Sold that and put it right into the condominium.

I love your idea Billy about staying out of debt. Once you're in debt that creates a spiral, you know?

Yeah. If you stay out of debt, you don't have to work half the time. You're closer to nature too.

How do you mean?

You're not a consumer. Like my yard. I don't spend a nickel's worth of time or money on maintaining my property, just 'cause of the woods.

("Not my ideal yard," I thought. But the woods are pretty.)

What year was this home built?

It's written in the concrete somewhere.

Do you need to do a new roof sometime soon?

I did one.

You already did one? When?

I put this Ondura® roof on. It's supposed to be a 50-year roof. It costs $50 a square, twice as much as a shingle roof. It's asphalt really. It's not shingles. It's corrugated asphalt. I put it right over the old roof. It's like twice as expensive as shingles. Pointing outside Billy said, "You can see it right there on that roof that covers my shop."

Aquarium/Kitchen Breakfast Bar, Billy Built in his Jacksonville Home
Madelyn Rubin

When I got home, I looked up Ondura® roofing on the Internet. It had some diverse reviews by users and professional roofers. The most helpful review was the following:

"Re: Ondura® Roofing [and Paint]
I have not used it personally but considered it strongly for roof replacements on some commercial property. This was 10-12 yrs. or so ago so the product

74

may be totally different now but at the time my personal concerns were about its ability to withstand impacts (limbs, heavy hail, edges breaking etc.) but was eventually talked out of it by some local contractors I know...if I remember correctly, they had seen problems with areas where it had been cut or screwed. On Edit, I began to feel somewhat conflicted because I had commented on something that you asked for personal experiences with and I offered why I chose not to use it. I began Googling "Ondura reviews" and there are a lot of forums online that offer opinions from actual users. After reading more than a few forums, there are customers saying it's great. However like most things in life, if a product moves a person to offer an opinion it is usually because of a problem, not because they were pleased. Of those offering opinions it looks like the majority of those users biggest problem is w/ peeling paint in the 5-10yr period after install. Deterioration around nail holes, stacks/vents and other cuts (what I was told by my friends) seems to be the next biggest issue. Almost everyone with a problem expressed great dissatisfaction with Ondura® warranty when they made claims. It appears from those willing to express their experiences of addressing the "lifetime warranty" is that Ondura® fights tooth and nail in actually making good on repair or replacement. The best solution that I read was that Ondura® offered a customer a 25% discount on their Ondura® brand paint w/ no labor reimbursement to repair a peeling problem for the customer. It was unclear if anyone else I read about actually ever received any support from Ondura® with their claim, just continual repeating that they are difficult to deal with.

That all said, you really need to read the forums for yourself, if you haven't already.

Darryl Kernopelli. 11-13-2009. Carterville, Illinois.
(Retrieved 10-9-2010)

Whenever a company has the above reputation in response to a customer wanting to put a claim against their warranty, I run for the hills. However, where you live usually affects roofing materials, so contact several local roofers who have used it and get references of those customers who have had it installed.

Back to my interview with Billy:
Billy, since you didn't take off the old roof, do you have to worry about wood rot? How about everybody else that has wood rot under the old roof?

It has to get pretty bad for someone not to want to put the new roof over the old roof. Your wood rot has to be there a long time. If it's just minor, it'll dry out and it'll be fine. Most roofers like tearing it off, because they can get more money for the job. But I think it's ridiculous not to put the new roof right over the old roof.

When I was a REALTOR®, we always encouraged tearing off the old roof, because of all the liability. We didn't want any problems in the future. If there is any wood rot, then you have the chance of termites. Then you have that issue to deal with. And it's so easy for them to come back on the REALTOR®. Anything that could be a problem, we always took extra care.

Billy added, "It's a lot easier to get a mortgage with a new roof too, isn't it?"

The mortgage is not the issue so much these days as the insurance. You have to get insurance to get a mortgage and most insurance companies won't give you insurance unless the roof is less than 15 years old.

"Billy," I continued, "so you said what you value most is that you've kept your freedom. What are your goals from here on out?"

Enjoy life, you know.

You're gona go down to the Keys and you're gona build that house. Is that to sell or use as a vacation home?

No, a vacation home. We're keeping it.

And y'all think you're gona live down there for a while?

Long enough to build it. Usually takes us about a year to build something.

Think you'll stay there for a while or you might come back up here?

No. Probably be back up here. It'll be a weekly rental and when it's not rented out, then I'll be able to enjoy it, you know.

Oh, it is gona be a weekly rental like ours is in Tallahassee. Okay! So y'all are gona furnish it too.

Un-huh. That's the only way I could afford it! I couldn't afford the taxes if I didn't rent it out.

And who are you gona get to help you get the furniture and stuff?

I don't know. Who knows how much furniture we'll have already? Yeah. I can tell you one thing. We won't be spending much on it.

You know, that gate that you and Timmy built at my old house in Mandarin years ago? It's still there and it's still beautiful and I'm still pissed off that I couldn't take it with me. So if you ever get bored one day and want to build a new one....it's so pretty with the trellises and the curly cued top.

"Was it all pressure treated wood?" Billy asked.

"Yeah," I answered.

Whenever I build a house now, I build it 100% pressure treated. I never worry about termites or rot or anything. This one, I didn't build it all out of pressure treated. I did the eves and the fascia. If you ever have to replace those boards, use pressure treated.

"You don't have to worry about the creosote"? I asked. I was always informed that the creosote that oozes from pressure treated wood is poisonous to people. You can smell it and feel it on your hands when you handle pressure treated wood.

"That's another lawyer thing," Billy replied. "Like our house down there that we built at the lake? It is all pressure treated."

"It's gona be around for a lonnnnng time," I said. "And you won't have to worry about termites."

"It'll be there forever"! Billy chimed in.

[Below is some information about the use of Pressure Treated Wood from the U.S. Environmental Protection Agency, 2011]:

Consumer Safety Information Sheet: Inorganic Arsenical Pressure-Treated Wood

CCA Table of Contents

Including Chromate Copper Arsenate (CCA), Ammoniacal Copper Arsenate (ACA), and Ammoniacal Copper Zinc Arsenate (ACZA)]

Consumer Information:

This wood has been preserved by pressure-treatment with an EPA-registered pesticide containing inorganic arsenic to protect it from insect attack and decay. Wood treated with inorganic arsenic should be used only where such protection is important.

Inorganic arsenic penetrates deeply into and remains in the pressure-treated wood for a long time. However, some chemical may migrate from treated wood into surrounding soil over time and may also be dislodged from the wood surface upon contact with skin. Exposure to inorganic arsenic may present certain hazards. Therefore, the following precautions should be taken both when handling the treated wood and in determining where to use or dispose of the treated wood.

Use-Site Precautions:

All sawdust and construction debris should be cleaned up and disposed of after construction.

Do not use treated wood under circumstances where the preservative may become a component of food or animal feed. Examples of such sites would be use of mulch from recycled arsenic-treated wood, cutting boards, counter tops, animal bedding, and structures or containers for storing animal feed or human food. Only treated wood that is visibly clean and free of surface residue should be used for patios, decks and walkways. Do not use treated wood for construction of those portions of beehives which may come into contact with honey.

Treated wood should not be used where it may come into direct or indirect contact with drinking water, except for uses involving incidental contact such as docks and bridges.

Handling Precautions:

Treated wood should not be burned in open fires or in stoves, fireplaces, or residential boilers because toxic chemicals may be produced as part of the smoke and ashes. Treated wood from commercial or industrial use (e.g., construction sites) may be burned only in commercial or industrial incinerators or boilers in accordance with state and Federal regulations. CCA-treated wood can be disposed of with regular municipal trash (i.e., municipal solid waste, not yard waste) in many areas. However, state or local laws may be stricter than federal requirements. For more information, please contact the waste management agency for your state.

Avoid frequent or prolonged inhalation of sawdust from treated wood. When sawing, sanding, and machining treated wood, wear a dust mask. Whenever possible, these operations should be performed outdoors to avoid indoor accumulations or airborne sawdust from treated wood.

When power-sawing and machining, wear goggles to protect eyes from flying particles. Wear gloves when working with the wood. After working with the wood, and before eating, drinking, toileting, and use of tobacco products, wash exposed areas thoroughly. Because preservatives or sawdust may accumulate on clothes, they should be laundered before reuse. Wash work clothes separately from other household clothing.

http://www.epa.gov/oppad001/reregistration/cca/cca_consumer_safety.htm

Last updated on Wednesday, February 16, 2011

Back to the Interview

Billy, what else do you want to do? You want to build a house in the Keys. Anything else?

"You know," Billy pondered, I'm trying to think if there's any place in the world that I'd like to travel to and visit. Seems like we have just about everything here in the states that everybody has overseas except for their cultures. If you want to see Grand Canyons or mountains, all these beautiful places here…if you like nature, right here there's plenty of places to go. If you want to visit people, I'm not that outgoing to go visit people that I don't know. There's a lot of people that are like that (outgoing) and I, kind of, admire them for it, like Lou (my brother)…but not me. I kind of like some of the architecture of the old places, cathedrals and everything, but they all seem like such a waste of money to me. I can respect the craftsmen that did it. I can see them in a picture. What's really cool about the Internet is I've gone through the Louvre, I've gone to many places….I've gone through Czechoslovakia and stuff. There's cameras everywhere! You can see whatever you want online now. It's not the same but you can go to Paris, you can go to the Champs-Elysees.

You have the Internet, of course.

"At Patty's house, not here" Billy clarified quickly. If she didn't have the Internet, then I would. I think it's that important. It saves me a lot of time going to the library, for one thing. But she has cable Internet and I'd have to deal with telephone Internet here cause it's TV too and I don't watch that much here. The only channel I watch is PBS.

You've got a cell phone?

Uh-Huh

Do I have that number? What's the number?

I don't know. It's John's cell phone really.

You pay for it?

Uh-huh. I pay $10 a month.

Cause it's an extra phone?

Uh huh. For him.

But it's a different number. It's your own number.

Right.

It was obvious that Billy didn't want to give me his phone number, probably for two reasons:

1. He thought that I might call too much and it would take some of his minutes away. However, since I am on T-Mobile too, it wouldn't cost anything for him to talk to me.

2. Most important, he doesn't like to talk much to people.

Billy, "He's only charging you $10 a month. That's a good deal," I said.

Yeah. It is a good deal. But he's always wanting to contact me and I never have a phone so.....

So, he said here! Laughing. But he did get you to pay $10 at least. Unlimited?

No, no.

500 minutes?

I don't think it's that much. There's actually 3 of us on the same plan.

You and him and his wife?

Yeah. And for me to contact him, it's free.

What phone company?

T-Mobile.

Oh, you can talk to anybody else who is on T-Mobile for free with T-Mobile.

Is that how it works? I'm not sure. He told me I could talk to him and his wife.

So he gets the bill and you pay him $10/month?

I pay him for a year at a time. I hate payments.

$120 a year.

But I would have Internet if I couldn't get it from my sister's.

So you just bring your laptop?

I use her laptop. She has about 3 of them. The school gives her laptops.

And you're not taking away from hers because you have wireless.

Right.

How about credit cards, Billy? Do you have any?

I have 2. One, Timmy and I have together. We keep the balance at zero. We never pay interest.

So you want to have some credit just in case?

I don't care about credit. I care about convenience. When I get gas, it's much easier to put in a card at the gas pump rather than going in the store and having to talk to somebody.

Does Timmy carry a credit balance?

Nobody in our family carries a balance except maybe one of us.

Anything else you want to say about anything?

"No", *Billy easily replied.*

I talked to Billy in the spring of 2010; I talked to him again in the fall of 2010. Lucky for me, they had not gone to the Keys, giving me a chance to get updated. Billy no longer had a phone. He got tired of answering it and being interrupted by its incessant ringing. He and Timmy are ok with their plans being delayed, as they have no one to answer to. Except, they are under a bit of pressure now. It took about 7 years for them to get a building permit to build the house on Marathon Key. It only lasts a limited period of time. Thus, they need to get the house started by Thanksgiving in order for the permit to remain valid. Also, Jessica, Timmy's daughter, is planning to start school in the Keys.

When I asked Timmy what Jessie thought about the move, he replied, "She doesn't care where she lives. She's fine with it."

Here are some notes from Billy after he got to the Keys:

From: bill
Sent: Saturday, January 15, 2011 3:40 PM
To: Madelyn rubin
Subject:

hey mag, i would try the recipe but i aint got 'lectricity. [I sent him a recipe].
have not had it for a couple of months and i found out that i do not need it. the
sun provides all that i need.
picture of the beach a half mile away that i walk to every morning at sunrise to
do my yoga. weather is perfect.

From: bill
Sent: Sunday, February 20, 2011 4:40 PM
To: madelyn rubin
Subject: RE: working on Book

mag, i think i was making between 25 to 30 k back then [in Jacksonville at
JEA.] i dont think that i even knew what i was making back then. this many
years later, it is surely a guess. it did not really matter and i didnt much

83

care. money was always much less important than freedom. the house is going well, should get a fresh supply of materials monday. will send pictures soon.

From: bill
Sent Fri 3/18/2011 7:46 AM

mag, i was at the mcdonalds at 630 am waiting for timmy to bring me a sausage biscuit. a guy came over to my table and gave me a bag of fruit yogurts and some crackers. i did not know what the deal was but i promptly thanked him. as he was walking away he said i could share it with my friends outside. apparently there are usually homeless people hanging out side. as i walked out the door, i noticed that they had not arrived yet. i enjoyed the yogurts. guess i am still a snappy dresser. i still eat breakfast there looking for a repeat performance. hope they don't notice me getting out of my airplane and driving to my million dollar home.

2012 Update:

I wanted to go and see Billy in the Keys ever since they started working on the house, a few years ago. I finally got the golden opportunity, Double Gold actually:
1. A good friend of mine was going to see a friend of hers in the same exact area. I wouldn't have to make the 8 hour drive by myself (I told you I was a wuss) and

2. Billy and Timmy had completed the house. Billy was living in it and putting on a few final touches. I wouldn't have to live on a boat for 4 days. (See, a wuss.)

Thus, I got to interview Billy again, having gone down to the Keys and which were more beautiful than I had remembered. It was great to see him and his brother Tim, and their gorgeous new home.

May 22, 2012

The last time we talked you were planning to come down here and live on the boat, you, Timmy and Jessie. But Jessie went back. How long was she here before she went back to your family home in Jacksonville?

She never came. She got an offer to go to an advanced placement school in Jax. Timmy as her father, myself and everybody else thought it would be a good idea for her to do that, so she stayed up in Jacksonville. It was advanced placement in academics. I guess her math and her reading skills are pretty high.

Who has worked with her mostly on her homework?

Since Timmy and I have been down here building this house, it's been her Aunt Patty.

How about when you all were up there?

Then it was everybody. Whoever she wanted to ask.

Did it depend on the subject?

Probably did. I fielded a lot of the math questions, but Timmy and Patty did too. In science, Patty's a geologist, so she would get earth science information from Patty. Patty also had tutored teachers in geology, so she would be a good person for that.

So, here I was sitting in Billy and Timmy's beautiful new Keys home. To summarize, they started the house in January, 2011, and Billy and Timmy built it from the ground up. The only thing they had anybody do was hire the concrete company to pour the foundation using those big concrete mixers. A homeless guy came by almost daily when they were working and said "anything, anything that y'all just hate to do, I'll do it. So they hired him to paint the entire house for an affordable hourly rate. And they would let the homeless guy stay in the unfinished house sometimes when the weather was bad. And now they and the homeless guy are friends. But the guy isn't your typical homeless guy. He hates homeless people who get food stamps. He likes to work for a living. He would just rather live in the woods and spend his money freely. But they had a falling out recently because the homeless guy was trying to push his religious beliefs and "save" Bill and Tim. Needless to say, they didn't agree with all of the guy's beliefs, and didn't feel particularly in need of salvation.

Everything else, Billy and Timmy did on their own to create this gorgeous home that has six sets of sliding glass doors. This is the type of home that "lovers of light" dream of. It took them about 14 months to build it. And they lived on the boat for one year and two months while building.

To bear the hot south Florida weather, Billy and Timmy would work in the western part of house in the a.m. and the eastern part of the house in the afternoon and evening. So, they even kept their bodies as energy efficient as possible throughout the process. Since they were shaded by trees in the East, even when there was not enough shade from the house, they used the trees to guide their building in the morning.

Bill and Tim's Keys home
Madelyn Rubin

Interview Continued with Billy, May, 2012:

So Billy, what was the easier part of living on the boat for 14 months and what was the hardest part?

We showered on the boat, but we didn't want to dump from the boat toilet into the canal, so every morning we would go to the beach park restroom facilities that are only half a mile away. We would clean up in their nice restroom facilities there and do our morning yoga on the beach. Timing was the only difficult part. We would have to wait sometimes till they opened up the park. But it wasn't that difficult.

The best part was watching things progress. And living on the boat. It's the first time we ever lived on a boat. It was kind of neat. When a big storm would come up, you could feel it hittin' the dock and blowin' around a bit. You'd have to make sure everything was tied down real well and it was kind of exciting.

The Boat
Madelyn Rubin

The friend of mine who is the homeless guy, who lives out in the woods...
a couple of nights he said he was terrified...seeing the wind hittin' the
trees, but it wasn't too bad most of the time...it was kind of nice.

So he lives in someone else's woods.

Yes. There are a lot of areas around here that are owned by the State of
Florida. A lot of properties are given to the State....or you could say the
State extorts it. Because, in order to get a building permit, if you give
them some land, they get you closer in line to get a permit. That's why it
took us 6 years to get a permit. We didn't have any land to give them and
couldn't afford $100,000 for a piece of land to give them.

*To find out more about the homeless guy, when you befriended him, you
weren't afraid he would ask to stay on your land or take advantage of
you?*

No, he's a nice guy. He stayed in the house when it wasn't finished a
couple of times to get out of the rain. As a matter of fact, when we got the
washer and dryer in, we let him do his laundry there a couple of times.

What if he wanted to come and stay under the carport now?

I wouldn't mind that.

Heavenly View from the Boat Dock
Madelyn Rubin

How about if people were renting the place out which you plan to do?

He wouldn't stay under the carport without asking first. He always asks. And on occasion, he would trade us some work to stay here.

He did a good job painting?

Yes, he is an EXCELLENT painter. In fact, the house that's being built now down the street, it is taking their painters weeks to paint that house. What they did in weeks, Steve did in two days. He knew what he was doing. Also, he wanted to learn how to do other stuff too. So when we were putting up the drywall, we would let him do a bit of labor. We worked with him.

In building this house, was there anything unique while building it compared to the other houses you've built in the past?

Yeah. In the past we've always built wood frame houses. This is a concrete block house. Makes it more valuable down here because of the hurricanes. Also, people feel a lot more secure with concrete block. It's somewhat more expensive but not a heck of a lot.

Anything else y'all did that was different with this house--you and Timmy being older?

Doing Yoga every day saved us on this house. We'd both be crippled if we hadn't done yoga every morning. If you skip it, you notice it. In my 50's, that's probably the best discovery that I've made. And it doesn't take very long. 10 minutes at most.

I think your Yoga program [by Peggy Cappy] took about 20 minutes. About the same time as my program by Swami Vidynand. [Yoga for Arthritis.]

I was thinking before that you were going to rent the home out for a few years before you decided to live here?

No, my plan has always been to live here and rent it out in interims. Stay in another place. Right now, I have a place down the street in a ground floor bedroom and bath in a friend's home. As an alternative, I could take our boat about 30 miles away to the other piece of property and stay on the canal beside it, in the boat.

You guys have done a beautiful job building this home. The hand built, hand milled, double toned wood cabinets are astonishingly beautiful. The design of 6 sliding glass doors, three on each level brings light into almost every corner. You can see the sun rise from the balconies. Everything is awesome! The game room. It is truly a paradise in paradise.

Is there a reason you built two stories rather than one?

Definitely. We wanted to take advantage of the ocean view you can see from the second story. This house is bigger than I wanted it to be. In order to take advantage of the better view, we went to 2000 sq.ft.

Last time I talked to you, you said you had been able to live on about $10,000 a year. Has that changed any? You'll be getting intermittent rent now. Will it stabilize your income?

I'll probably continue to live on $10,000 a year.

Hand Milled, Hand Built Double Toned Kitchen Cabinets by Bill and Tim
Madelyn Rubin

The big difference here is that you're not pooling your money for meals with the rest of your family. That should affect your income some.

Yeah. It might be cheaper for me to live down here. I was pooling my food up there, but I have simpler tastes, I eat simpler meals down here.

Rather than somebody like me who comes in and buys a bunch of fruit, eggs, bacon, waffles, salad stuff and more.

Third Floor Bedroom, Overlooking the Canal
Madelyn Rubin

Absolutely. I have modest tastes. I could eat a peanut butter and jelly sandwich or a hummus and egg sandwich every day. I can eat it for supper.

"Yeah, well, I would eat it for supper every day if I was in jail," I replied assuredly. Peanut butter and jelly maybe, but not hummus and egg.

You haven't even tried it!

That's because they're too similar. I like to have something that has some variation; they're both too smooth. I would like Hummus and Granola or Hummus and crackers.

Well, you have some weird tastes. [Pot calling the kettle black.] Timmy loves it. I'm not alone.

So anything unique happen while you were building this house?

Gorgeous Sunrise from the new Keys House
Madelyn Rubin

Yeah. This house is a lot more complex than other houses, mainly due to government intervention. They want to know every single thing that you do so that they can get a piece of the action. I waited for the permit for the dock, it came in, then I had to wait for the permit for the house, then the permit for the dock expired. Then I had to reapply for the permit for the dock again. It took a year again to re-permit the dock. And it always costs more money. And they won't allow you to build the dock until you have the house permit. Catch 22. The feds, the state and the county won't work together with each other. You have to be the intermediary between all these organizations and they each have individual paperwork done to their own standards. Just to get the permits for renting the place took **months**! And to figure it out, you'd go to the city who said they want this document and you'd ask, where do I get that? And they'd say. "We don't know, you have to go to the state." The state says "we don't know you have to go to the county." You keep jumpin from hoop to hoop trying to figure out what each one of them wants. That's the biggest struggle, permitting and filling in all of their little paperwork details. Other counties have been a little difficult but they don't know the half of where the real paperwork starts. Building the house was the easiest part of the whole job.

Needless to say, this is the type of Wrench that really irks Billy. Having to deal with bureaucrats and lawyers bothers him more than anything. He

93

sees, so well, the puffing up of each bureaucracy in order to maintain themselves and the loss of their original purpose: to help and protect people in their jurisdiction. I think he gets upset with lawyers for the same reason. If people just talk to each other reasonably, there is no need for lawyers. He's very reasonable. For me, maybe I've been around a lot more unreasonable people, because I value lawyers very much....knowing how unreasonable and greedy some people can be.

Back to the interview:
So if you didn't have a dock where did you put your boat?

We built the dock anyway even though we didn't have the permit. When we first moved down here we thought we had the permit so we built enough of the dock to get to the water. Then the city came and shut us down. They said we had to have this permit. When we showed them our dock permit, they said, "No, it's expired. And you don't have OUR permit." They each have their own permit. Each permit is a few thousand bucks too. We had the Federal permit by the Army corps of Engineers but we didn't have the city's permit. It cost us more for the permits than it cost us to build the dock.

At least, you got the dock done though so you could get back and forth to the boat to eat and sleep and get stuff you needed out of it.

Yeah. It was great! I wouldn't have done it any differently I don't think.

How about in terms of food? You have a stove on the boat?

We have a microwave on the boat. Most of our meals would be done on the microwave rather than use the stove because we had a gas stove. It was just easier to microwave everything.

So your typical lunch was…

We had all kinds of stuff. Sometimes we would go to Subway or Publix and split a Sub.

[*Now these are two guys are about 5'11' weighing about 180 lbs. each. They MUST have gotten the 24 inch subs and split them!*]

They're delicious. Sometimes we'd get a roast chicken at Publix. They'd be on sale for $5 bucks. We have a little refrigerator on the boat. We had everything we needed there except for a toilet. And we had a toilet, but we didn't use it.

Did anybody ever say anything to you at the park about going there to wash up every morning?

No, not at all. On occasion, they'd be closed. The policeman who lived right next door to the gate to the beach park was the one who had the responsibility to open it every morning. Sometimes he wouldn't be on time. Right before we had the toilets up and running here at the house, the policeman at the park said, "You know, if I'm not here, and this gate isn't open, you can always come through OUR gate. I guess they finally got to know us and trust us. They knew we wanted to go to the beach and do our exercises…

Thinking of all of the construction sites I have been around in my life as a former REALTOR® and remembering the loud radios, each with their own preferred blaring sounds, I had to ask the most pressing question on my mind, "So did you guys have the radio on while you and Timmy worked?" I figured this would be the REAL test as to how different Billy was from other people who built houses.

"No, we didn't even have a radio here," Billy said, having no idea of the thoughts of blaring radios going through my head.

If you had to do it all over again, would you have done anything differently?

Yeah. I'd always do stuff differently. We originally planned on making the upstairs deck like the downstairs deck, just a regular wood deck. Then we decided we would rather seal off the upstairs deck so the downstairs deck could be protected from the rain. So we put plywood on the upstairs deck and waterproofed it. But we had already put all of the structure in before we changed our minds, so it doesn't have a slope and retains water. So we would have put a couple of inches of slope to let the water runoff. Outside of that…. oh, and probably, before I spent $3 on each of the window shades, I would have had Madelyn down here to tell me to spend $30 each on some nice ones. (Laugh!!!)

How did you arrange with your Cousin Lisa (my niece, Lisa), to get free furniture for five rooms, including accessories? I know she has access to furniture. She just has it all stored somewhere?

Yeah. Some of the furniture was in the condominiums that she has managed for 20 years. People have died or were getting rid of old furniture. As a matter of fact, while we were up there, some lady calls and says she's getting a queen sized bed and she wanted to get rid of the one that she had. That's the one in the master bedroom that we have. It's in great shape and it looks like it's brand new. She might have gone to a king size, I don't know.

Furniture Lisa Provided for the Keys House
Madelyn Rubin

So Lisa has a bunch of stuff in storage, just in case someone else needs something.

People are always giving it away. They're all rich people changing stuff, so Lisa comes by and gets rid of it for them. She has about 4 garages that are all just full of furniture. They're garages of the condos that haven't been bought yet. It'll only last until next December, because then she's no longer the broker there, so she has to get rid of the stuff in the garages.

So you had a choice of furniture?

Yeah. Some of it was choice.

You and Timmy took the cost of this home out of your savings, so then you're going to reinvest your money when you rent the home out. Do you have a goal of NOT renting it out in the future and just living in it permanently when you get a certain amount of money? Do you like renting it out a few days or weeks, then living in it for a few weeks?

I don't know. I haven't done it yet. [Laugh]. If it's an income, it's always nice to have an income. Previously, I just lived off of savings from stuff that we built or whatever [investing in stocks]. I do need 10 more Quarters to get social security. I'm not sure when I'm gona do that yet. I could pay a portion of this as part of my social security income or I could even get a job. A friend of mine's been asking me about doing some engineering for power plants. They have outages and need stuff fixed in the plants. They're always looking for engineers.

Would you do it part time? (I know Billy hasn't had a 9-5 job for decades; it is hard for me to imagine him working this type of job.)

If I did that job, I'd have to do it full time for a few months at a time. Plant outages last for a few months.

Would you rather live that time here at your new home or would you just as soon be living on your boat? [Billy plans to rent the home out intermittently and to live in it for 6 months or intermittently.]

If I was working, I'd be away from here. I'd rent this out while I was gone. The only problem is that the city has these special regulations where you have to be in town when you rent out a home. So I don't want to do something illegal. I could get John [Billy's brother who live ½ an hour away] to watch out for it.

Back to the house, what are your electric bills for this 2000 square foot home in the hot Florida Keys?

They've been about $20 a month.

But you haven't run the CH&A.

I never run the AC. I just open all of the doors up to the ocean breeze.

What is the R factor in the walls?

R30 in the ceilings. For a concrete block house it's VERY well insulated. But a concrete house is, usually, not very well insulated. In fact, the inspector said he's never seen a house as tight as this one for a concrete block house. Usually your furring strips are on the inside of the house using 1" bys whatever is needed. You put ¾ inch foam insulation between all the furring strips. Instead, we took 1.5 inch thick foam, put it on the walls, then put the furring strips on top of it, nailed through the furring strips into the foam and into the concrete. So it was just solid foam underneath it. We have the insulation of the solid foam, plus we have a ¾ air gap for the furring strip, then the ½ inch drywall inside of that. We always put as much insulation as we can. It's imperative for anybody that's energy conscious at all--or money conscious.

For the ceiling, you just put in the regular rolled insulation?

Yeah. Down here, they don't use much insulation. I don't know why. In the floors, sometimes they don't put any. We put R30 in the floors too [the home is off grade].

You installed another homemade solar water heater in this home? Where did you get the hot water tank this time?

A friend of mine had two solar hot water panels at her house. She got rid of them and replaced them because they stopped working years ago. She gave them to me because she figured I could use them, so I stored them. That was another problem down here. Here, they require that you specify all of the products that you are using. A manufacturer will get on the "good list" for the state and say, "here is our product, and it's been tested."

So you have to buy their exclusive product. I had this beautiful solar hot water collector. I had no specifications on it at all. I could calculate what it is capable of, which I ended up doing. I looked through the Internet to find something that looked just like it. When I found something that matched, I told them that was what I had or that was what I was buying. And it is the same thing. So it was approved. Then I used a standard hot water heater, 40 gallon. I mounted the solar collector at the bottom of the roof and built a box in the attic for the hot water heater that was a little bit above the solar collector on the roof. If you mount the hot water heater above the solar collector, then you don't have to have any pumps, no noise because there's no electricity involved. It's natural convection. The hot water will go up into your tank. The cold water in your tank will go down into the solar collector. It works perfectly.

So once again, Billy, along with his business partner and brother, Timmy, used the expertise that they have developed over the last 50 years to fulfill another dream...have a solid, beautiful home in the Florida Keys. Billy started his life-long learning with his parents, then continued it through formal education and research, research and more research... first in the libraries, then on the Internet. He used a penetrating and driving initiative, one that was drawn from a desire to be free. Free from anyone telling him what, when, where, or how long he had to work. Free to do what he wants, when, where and how. Free to get what he wants. Free to choose the things that life offers rather than feel that he must do things because they are dictated by media, advertisements, Wall Street or by anyone else. Billy has actually taken our American motto literally: that we all live in the "land of the free."

Almost Finished Exterior of the Keys House
Madelyn Rubin

Making It Happen for You and Your Family

While I know it can be more difficult to take Billy's ideas and use them, when you have a spouse and family, many of Billy's ideas can still work. It's a state of mind. It's the desire to be free from the constant barrage of media telling you what you need and having the feeling that you must keep up with the Joneses.

Also, I understand that when Billy started his life plan in the 70's, it was much easier in the United States to get an education, get a job, make money and save money. When I watched Alex Gibney's excellent film, *Park Avenue: Money, Power and the American Dream* (2012) on Netflix® this year, the changes in our economy from the 1970's until now-second decade of the 21st century, became crystal clear. Based on this documentary and many other sources I've come across, since the 1970's the very rich (now known as the "Top 1 %") have been getting richer and the rest of us, the 99%, have been static or getting poorer. It is also apparent that the 1% have tight control of our major fiscal institutions, much of our media, and our Congress, not to mention many state governments. The ability of the 99% to control our economic future is much diminished and difficult. The wealthy 1% has the money and the power to pass laws that make themselves richer and to pass other laws that make the 99% poorer and more powerless. The 1% can pay for puppet politicians who can be manipulated to do the biding of their puppet masters. They are able, with their vast wealth, to carefully choose who shall be supported for local, state and federal positions.

The *Park Avenue* documentary notes that education is still the key to getting out of the cycle of poverty and powerlessness, however, with the cost of a college degree going up approximately 500% since the 1970's, obtaining a four-year degree is now very, very difficult, if not impossible. The film *Park Avenue* is a cautionary tale about wealth and power and how we must be so careful about who we vote into office, and how we all must understand and research how their votes will affect *us*. Don't take their political rhetoric at face value. If you support education and creating real jobs for most people, are you voting for the politicians that have actually voted for these issues? Look for the proof.

Even with our great country's social, economic, and governmental struggles, I still think we can make the necessary changes to ensure our survival and growth, and I use Billy as a role model for our growth, in many ways. Over the last year, with a fresh, and flexible state of mind, my husband and I have reduced our monthly expenses and reduced our debt tenfold. While we never expected to be able to retire, even with social security, we are now, happily, in a state of semi-retirement. Though we can actually foresee full retirement with only a few final debts to be paid, we will continue to work part-time. The joy in this process: soon we won't *have* to make ends meet… we will just *want to* continue to work for fun and the social good.

Although more typical of most Americans than innovative people like Billy, my husband and I have made the following changes to help us become, like Billy, free and independent from debt and unnecessary obligation.

The changes my husband and I have made in our lives are the following:

1. Because of the fact that we have set up weekly financial meetings to review our bank statements and budget, we know exactly how much we have to work, part-time, to take those extra trips we want, etc.

2. We both receive Social Security retirement benefits, so we have a base income to work with. Otherwise, we would both have to work more.

3. We discuss any small or large purchases that we want to make that are not in our budget, before we make them.

4. We assess bills weekly to determine whether we want to work harder to keep what extra money provides for us, e.g. we review the details of our cell phone bill and our cable internet/television bill. These companies offer "specials" regularly, so we contact them every few months to make sure we are getting the most service for our money. We dropped data service on our cell phones for a few months until T-Mobile included data service and Internet for the same price that we had been paying without it. We don't

have to work so hard this way. We also take advantage of Affiliation (i.e. teacher, nurse, etc.) discounts, Senior Citizen discounts and military discounts, which most companies offer. <u>Always</u> ask!

5. We took advantage of the current lower mortgage rates and refinanced the mortgage balance on our home in order to have a smaller monthly payment and not have to work so hard. Billy would probably rather pay off a mortgage, but refinancing has worked very well for us. We didn't take any "cash back", which would have increased the mortgage balance…and the payments.

6. We also refinanced our two rental properties with the lower mortgage rates. For the first time, we have enough cash flow to be able to pay for rental repairs without working more, or putting it on a credit card. When the repairs are completed, we'll use the cash flow to save in a separate fund for future rental repairs, major and minor.

7. Whenever possible, we are making our own repairs. Rather than spend $2000 to paint a home, we are painting it ourselves (along with my sister, who is willing to do it for an affordable price.) Added bonus: it provides exercise for us and more time to be with loved ones.

8. We have found an awesome pharmacy from India where we can get the prescriptions we need filled for 20-40% of the price locally. (Note: make sure your "offshore" pharmacy is selling real and not low-potency or counterfeit drugs. A personal referral from a health professional is excellent, or check online to see how other customers feel about the company.

9. We do most of our own lawn care and our own house cleaning now and get more exercise.

10. We are committed to paying our credit cards down to zero and keeping them paid off. That will save us about $70 a month in interest. We are using any tax refunds to pay down the credit cards

rather than having fun with the funds. Short term sacrifice for the long term gain.

11. "Tricked" again. Recently, I saw that I was only 200 points on our credit card "rewards program" from getting 20,000 points and receiving $200 that we would apply toward our credit card balance. So, my husband and I decided to use our credit card for normal items so that we could get those points. We agreed to pay it right back to the credit card company that very month. Low and behold, before we knew it, we had borrowed $800 on our credit card that month. The worst part was that we didn't have the money to pay the $800 back within that month. Do you know why? I was stunned when I realized it. On the one hand, we were using our credit card generously. On the other hand, I thought that we had "extra money" in the bank account because we had paid for routine items with the credit card rather than with our cash in the bank. But we didn't connect the two. "Oh, we have some extra money this month," we thought. "I'll landscape an area in the yard I've been wanting to improve." We had totally blocked out the fact that we would have to pay the much higher balance on the credit card this month. Thus, we would have needed to save a lot more money in our bank account than we did. We left ourselves short. That is what the credit card companies hope we all do. A higher balance gives them more interest and tightens their hold on you.

I don't think we are very different from many people in the country. We want to think we have more money in our bank accounts, so when it looks like we do, we spend it.

12. We plan and prepare our own meals a lot more. Doing this, we save hundreds of dollars a month. We also get more exercise walking around the kitchen. We get more time together if we cook with each other. An added value is that we are eating healthier.

13. We search for "buy one, get one free" coupons for our favorite restaurants.

14. Those weekly meetings help us to keep our overspending habits in check by reviewing all of our bills, credit cards and bank accounts everytime.

15. I love going on a spending spree at our local mall. My weakness is blouses. I still get them, but I just scale-down. I buy a blouse on sale for $10 to $15 once every couple of months. I bought three beautiful, shapely t-shirts this month for $15.00 total. It's something I look forward to because it doesn't happen as often as it used to.

16. We barter when we can. As a photographer, if a vendor we use has a need for photographs for their family, or to use as a gift, I barter. We still have to pay Uncle Sam, but there is less money outflow by using more sweat equity.

17. We maintain a separate bank account for items that we need to save for and for bills that are not paid monthly, such as auto repairs, medical bills, travel, and vet bills. Then, we aren't surprised and panicked when urgent bills come-due.

18. We have shared our new lifestyle with our friends and family members. That way, they don't ask us meet them at expensive restaurants. Instead they have us over for dinner or we have them over for dinner. Or we go to a restaurant where we have coupons.

19. We pay $8.50 a month for instant, streaming Netflix® movies at home. Now, we rarely go to the movies.

20. We bought a solar water heater and have saved 30% on our electric bill every month. It used to run around $300 a month and now it runs around $200 a month.

21. The toughest decision we made was when we decided to cancel my health insurance. My husband is on a Medicare Advantage program so it wasn't a problem for his insurance. The cost is included in his Social Security benefit. But, for me, we thought about my insurance long and hard and figured out just how much less we would have to work and where we could spend this extra

$320 a month. This choice isn't for people that have a high medical risk situation, or for children. But it's a conscious choice we made. Rather than keeping health insurance, I have committed to eating healthier and to doing yoga at least every other day. We're still taking a chance. When affordable health care insurance (the Affordable Healthcare Act) is available, I will enroll and pay 35% of what it *was* costing me. We cancelled my insurance at this point because it gives us so much more freedom and happiness to spend this big chunk of money taking vacations.

22. Working together like this has given us an unexpected added bonus: we feel closer to each other because we are actively working together to improve the quality of our lives.

It's a freeing experience to live really free for the first time in our lives.

www.ingramcontent.com/pod-product-compliance
Lightning Source LLC
Chambersburg PA
CBHW020510030426
42337CB00011B/310